Reichstag Fire : ashes of democracy

Reichstag Fire: ashes of democracy

R John Pritchard

Editor-in-Chief: Barrie Pitt
Editor: David Mason
Art Director: Sarah Kingham
Picture Editor: Robert Hunt
Designer: Michael Frost
Cover: Denis Piper
Special Drawings: John Batchelor
Photographic Research: Benedict Shephard
Cartographer: Richard Natkiel

Contents

Funeral of the Weimar Republic

Introduction by Sydney L Mayer

Political trials are not only a Twentieth Century phenomenon; they have been going on for many centuries. They seldom have achieved the ends at which those who staged them aimed. When Martin Luther was tried for heresy in the Sixteenth Century, although he was found guilty, his reform movement within the Church was publicized to the extent that it broke the unity of Western Christendom. The trial of Warren Hastings in the late Eighteenth Century did not tarnish the reputation of India's first governor-general in the light of history; although it broke his career at the time, he appears today as one of the builders of modern India. In our own century, show trials of a political nature often have backfired in the long run. Stalin's purges of the 1930s may have rid the Soviet Union of the enemies of Stalin. But they disenchanted a generation of idealistic socialists in the West who had seen Russia as a model experimental state. The trial of Van der Lubbe in 1933 by

Nazi Germany, in much the same way, did not serve the purposes intended. Nobody now, and few people at the time, believed the Nazis' story that Van der Lubbe was the agent of the Communists, who allegedly used him to burn the Reichstag. Ironically, it is the political counter-trial staged by the Communists that is still widely believed. The Communists stated that it was in fact the Nazis who used Van der Lubbe to destroy the greatest monument to democratic government in the Weimar Republic as part of a plan to discredit democratic institutions in general and the bankrupt régime the Nazis replaced in particular; then, according to the Communist story, the Nazis double-crossed poor Van der Lubbe, tried him, and executed him, placing the blame for the fire on the Communists.

In the Second World War the Allies painted everything that Nazi Germany did in dark colors for the sake of propaganda. This attitude has continued since 1945 in view of the

revelations of the atrocities committed by Hitler's Germany which were exposed at the end of the war and since. One has tended to disbelieve anything the Nazis said about themselves. Only recently has this postwar attitude been modified. Recent studies have shown that in the case of the Reichstag Fire the Nazis were, at least, partly right. Fritz Tobias has proven to the satisfaction of many that Van der Lubbe started the fire after all, that he did so alone, and that the Nazis' charges of conspiracy as well as the Communists' were false. But even Tobias's findings have not closed the case of the Reichstag Fire. An international committee was formed to disprove the Tobias thesis, and their recent findings, supported by even Germany's present Chancellor, Willy Brandt, conclude that the Nazis conspired to burn the Reichstag, agreeing to a large measure with the Communists' thesis of the 1930s. Back to square one, it would seem. It is always difficult for the historian of

A communist rioter is buried. Germany is tearing herself to pieces, and the Reichstag Fire is Hitler's cue for the leap into dictatorship

recent events to separate myth from reality. Did Van der Lubbe really start the Reichstag Fire? If so, was he the tool of the Nazis or the Communists? Or did he do it alone without reference to either? Or was Van der Lubbe innocent? R John Pritchard takes up each of these suppositions and critically analyzes them all. In the end he proves that old suspicions and critical attitudes die hard. But he leaves little doubt about the mystery of the Reichstag Fire. If the Nazis did not burn the Reichstag, as John Pritchard claims, they certainly were quick to make use of it for their short-term political aims. The flames which consumed the Reichstag symbolically devoured the remnants of a democratic Germany as well. Perhaps the trial of Van der Lubbe was the last fair trial while Hitler was in power.

'The Reichstag is Burning!'

On Monday 27th February 1933, Rudolf Scholz is the night watchman at the German Reichstag building, which houses the German Parliament. Like many other employees at the Reichstag, he has worked there faithfully for many years and is a virtual fixture of the place. As he begins his nightly rounds in the enormous building, he punches his time clock. It registers 8.10pm. At this time every entrance except the north, Portal Five, is supposed to be closed, since the Reichstag is not in session.

Scholz takes his duties seriously this night, as any other. Like many men who have become accustomed to a lifetime of dull, tedious occupations, he prides himself on his attention to details. His appointed task is to turn off all lights and to make sure that every door and window is securely latched after the deputies have gone home. Such is his usual care that he generally takes about half an hour to finish his nightly circuit of inspection.

While Inspector Scholz makes the rounds, Albert Wendt, a lugubrious-looking individual with an enormous walrus moustache. is night porter at Portal Five, Wendt receives a request to put through a telephone call from Erich Birkenhauer, a communist journalist from Essen, to Ernst Torgler, the chairman of the Reichstag communist faction. Because the outside switchboard closed at 8pm, Torgler comes down to take the call in Wendt's presence. Later Wendt would recall that Torgler promised to meet someone at a restaurant. It is still a very dull evening. The time is 8.20.

In the meantime, Rudolf Scholz has found nothing unusual. Security precautions at the Reichstag were always vigilantly maintained, but the Reichstag staff has been especially careful in observing them in the last several months owing to a recent investigation of all security regulations when someone stole a valuable document from the archives. Besides, Rudolf Scholz is aware of the political tensions in the air; while he is preoccupied with private thoughts tonight, he overlooks nothing—especially anything which appears out of the ordinary.

At approximately 8.30, Scholz arrives at the Plenary, or Parliamentary Sessions Chamber. Making sure that everything is correctly in order, he starts to continue. But as he leaves his sharp ears pick up the sound of footsteps on the rich carpeting. He snaps on the lights to see who is there. It is only Miss Anna Rehme, the group secretary for the communists. Answering Scholz's questions, Miss Rehme explains that one of the communist deputies, Wilhelm Koenen, who is also the Secretary-General of the German Communist Party, has requested that she bring some election materials to the Communist Party chambers upstairs. After exchanging a few additional pleasantries, Scholz continues on with his inspections, but he takes note of the time: 8.32. He completes his rounds a few minutes later, at 8.35, finishing at the north entrance, Portal Five. While he prepares himself to go home, he chats idly with Wendt.

Soon Torgler, Koenen, and Miss

Above: Ernst Torgler, Chairman of the German Communist Party's Reichstag Delegation.*Right:* The Plenary Sessions Chamber of the German Reichstag

Rehme join them. Torgler gives his keys to Scholz, and they indulge in some light conversation. Torgler and his companions leave at 8.38. They are the last deputies to leave the Reichstag, and there is absolutely nothing unusual in the way they leave; they certainly give no sign of being in flight. Anna Rehme is obese and suffers from varicose veins, so they make their way very slowly. Talking quietly, the trio walk along the River Spree embankment to the Friedrichstrasse Station, where Anna Rehme leaves them. Torgler and Koenen continue on to the Friedrichstrasse branch of Aschinger's Restaurant, a respectable place where Torgler and Koenen are well-known. There they join Birkenhauer for dinner as arranged earlier. The three sit together in a quiet corner, and Torgler orders beef broth, stewed kidneys, raw hamburger, and beer. They talk until around 10.00 when an obviously excited head waiter comes over to their table and asks whether they have already heard that the Reichstag is on fire. They look at each other in astonishment and rise to their feet. 'Are you crazy?' says Torgler, 'That's impossible!'

Meanwhile, at the Reichstag, Rudolf Scholz finally leaves for home at around 8.40, and Albert Wendt remains alone by the door. At 8.45 he records the arrival of Willi Otto, the Reichstag postman, who empties the letter boxes at the Reichstag Post Office in the gallery every night. By 8.55 Willi Otto, too, leaves the Reichstag, again passing through Portal Five. The entire building is bathed in complete silence; a whisper would echo the length of the house.

Outside the Reichstag Berlin is freezing cold; the thermometer reads 22 degrees Fahrenheit. An icy wind blows briskly out of the east throwing up whitecaps on the River Spree which curves along closely under the Reichstag's northeast tower. Because the Reichstag is not in session, the streets nearby are lighted very dimly, and dark shadows consequently mantle the exterior walls. Those few hardy souls still on the lonely streets hasten homeward under clear skies. Beyond an occasional crunch of footsteps on the snowy pavement or the distant clatter of a tram, there is little to disturb the quiet of the

wintry night.

Mrs Elfriede Kuesner, who is on her way to the National Club, by chance happens to notice a man darting out of the shadows of Portal Two, the South Entrance, but later it will be firmly established that he was taking cover from the wind by standing in the doorway and jumping out to catch his bus when it arrived. It will also be determined that this fleeting incident occurred at 8.55, at the same time that Willi Otto was leaving the north entrance.

At 9.08 Hans Flöter, a student of theology and philosophy, approaches the southwest corner of the Reichstag from the adjoining Tiergarten. He is on the way home after a day spent working in the Eastern Reading Room of the State Library on Unter den Linden. He heads across the Königs-platz, parallel to the great ramp on the west side of the building. He passes the Grand Entrance on this side of the Reichstag, which is dignified by an imposing central portico upheld by six massive columns. A huge inscription across the beam at the top of the

The west front of the Reichstag in the 1920 s

portico dedicates the building 'To the German People'. The Grand Entrance is flanked on either side by an exterior wall with three rows of five windows, each recessed deeply between other columns. In front of the portico a wide flight of steps leads down to the Bismarck Memorial in the Königs-platz, and halfway between the memorial and the Grand Entrance the great carriageway bisects the line of steps.

As Hans Flöter passes below the portico, he can hear his own footsteps echoing across the icy open square. Suddenly he is startled by a sound of splintering glass. His first thought is that some stupid custodian has clums-ily broken a window. But just then he again hears glass shattering twice more. He spins around in time to see a dark figure crouching in a deep bal-cony beside the first floor where the Reichstag Restaurant is located. Flöter has to look very high because he is situated far below on a level with the Bismarck Memorial, but he sees the dark shape strike a match and then bend its body through the open window into the restaurant. Flöter runs left towards the north side of the building in search of a policeman, and

in doing so he almost collides with Police Sergeant Karl Buwert beyond the great ramp. Flöter cries out, 'Someone is breaking into the Reichstag!'

The policeman seems to hesitate, and the excited student gives Buwert a resounding whack on the back to get the sergeant moving. Without looking back Buwert runs up the steps and peers at the ground floor windows over the edge of the balustrade. After mobilizing Buwert, Flöter hurries to his nearby home at 4a Hindersinstrasse for dinner; the weather is too cold for him to stay outside.

Meanwhile Werner Thaler, a typesetter, has come round the corner from Simonstrasse just as Flöter finds Buwert. Thaler is on his way from Brandenburg Gate to the Lehrter Station. He, too, hears the breaking glass, and he runs up to the inclined drive to see more closely. Then he climbs on top of the curved stone balustrade and stares into the half-light. He sees two men on the balcony but no torches. He immediately runs off for a policeman whom he has seen earlier south of the building.

Thaler cannot find the policeman, so he shouts into the darkness for help and then speeds back towards the Grand Entrance. Seconds later he meets Buwert, who by this time has been joined by another young man in a black coat and top boots. The three men gawk foolishly at the bizarre sight of a flickering light moving to and fro behind a frosted window on the first floor. Then suddenly the flame races toward the southern corner of the building, and it can be seen darting from one window to the next. The men outside run after it until they reach the last window. There it momentarily pauses. Thaler, recovering first, screams, 'Shoot, man, shoot!' Buwert draws his revolver and, finally convinced that the intruder is intent upon arson, fires blindly through the window. The mysterious fire disappears from sight as the window shatters. The total elapsed time from Flöter's arrival at the scene to Buwert's shot has been just slightly over two minutes.

A few moments after Sergeant Buwert's gunfire, two married couples, a salesman by the name of Karl Kuhl and his spouse, and a bookbinder, Hermann Freudenberg and his wife, happen to approach the Reichstag from the Königsplatz. While still some distance away, they notice a glimmering of fire through the windows on the ground floor of the Reichstag. Quickly running toward the carriageway ramp they shout, 'Police! Fire!' By the time they reach the ramp they see one heavy drapery after another erupt into leaping, writhing flames behind the glass. Buwert, hearing them approach, requests Kuhl and Freudenberg to ring the fire alarm. They run off down the Simsonstrasse with Mrs Freudenberg to activate the first fire-box they can find. At last they spot the German Engineering Institute, at the corner of Friedrich Ebertstrasse and Dorotheenstrasse. Ramming their way past the people coming out of the building after a course that ended at 9.00, they breathlessly hail the custodian, Otto Schaeske: 'The Reichstag is burning! Call the Fire Brigade!'

Schaeske is staggered by the news, but he numbly reaches for the telephone book as he gapes in astonishment. His fingers fumble blindly through the pages until Emil Luck, who is helping him in the cloakroom, grabs the book and finds the correct number. Luck dials the number and gives the first fire alarm of the evening. The call is received at Fire Brigade Headquarters at 9.13. Within one minute the alarm is issued from there to Brigade Section Six at the Linienstrasse Fire Station which responds rapidly. Less than four minutes after receiving the alarm, the first fire engines, under the direction of Chief Fire Officer Emil Puhle, screeches to a halt in front of the Reichstag northwest tower by the ramp. They cannot drive up the rampway because their tires skid on the thin sheet of ice and snow covering the stone pavement. By 9.19 another unit from Section Seven arrives, commanded by Fire Officer Waldemar Klotz; it was sent in response to a separate alarm. At first there is some confusion as the firemen rush from one door to another, finding entrances locked, not knowing that only the north entrance, Portal Five, is open. Ladders are quickly thrown up against the walls, however, and al-already hoses lace the carriageway ramp by 9.20. At the same time two fire boats steam carefully down the River Spree in gloomy darkness to add their efforts in containing the blaze.

Meanwhile Sergeant Buwert's first instinct is to find help. He asks the young man in the black coat to spread the alarm to the Brandenburg Gate Police Station. 'Tell them,' he says, 'the Reichstag is burning and to call the Fire Brigade.' The young man does as he is told, but Buwert, who has a general distrust of civilians, repeats the order to a Reichswehr soldier who comes up a minute later. The soldier agrees, but Buwert is no sooner out of sight than the soldier catches a bus instead. Meanwhile Sergeant Buwert's shots have also attracted the attention of two other policemen who race up from the Siegesallee. Buwert quickly orders one of them to sound the fire alarm in the Moltkestrasse. This is the second fire alarm of the evening, the one calling Waldemar Klotz and Section Seven.

A moment later Constable Helmut Poeschel appears; he was quietly patrolling near the northeast corner of the Reichstag when Buwert fired his gun. The time is 9.15. Now, startled, he hears Buwert bellow, 'Fire! Tell the Porter at Portal Five!' Poeschel runs off to do that, arriving a minute later at the north entrance. There his shouting brings Albert Wendt outside, but Wendt seems completely thick-witted at first. Poeschel knows that a fire alarm is located in the porter's lodge, but

Wendt will not sound an alarm unless he can verify the fire for himself. After carefully locking the door behind him, Wendt rushes down the pavement without his coat or hat to see for himself. Turning the corner, he runs up the inclined ramp. To his horror he can see the entire glass dome of the Reichstag already glowing in the dark, flickering red from the flames far beneath. Already a crowd of spectators is assembling. Hearing the Fire Brigade has already been called, Wendt dashes back to his lodge at Portal Five in order to warn all of the Reichstag senior staff whom he can reach by telephone. His first attempts to reach Chief Engineer Eugen Mutzka and Chief House Inspector Alexander Scranowitz in their official apartments nearby are in vain; in his excitement he probably misdials the correct numbers. Still trying by 9.19 he finally contacts Eduard Prodöhl, the Chief Reichstag Messenger, and Paul Adermann, the night porter at the Speaker's residence. Adermann in turn telephones the Director of the Reichstag, Privy Councillor Galle, and the Prussian Ministry of the Interior just over 300 yards away from the Reichstag on Unter den Linden where the call is taken by Göring's secretary, Miss Grundtmann. She in turn passes the message to Göring's adjutant, Police Captain Jacoby, who tells Göring. Göring has been upstairs talking with Ludwig Grauvert, the Under Secretary of the Prussian Interior. Göring is dumbfounded and cries, 'What the hell is going on? Get me a car! Now! I'm going straight there!'

Meanwhile Scranowitz, hearing the ruckus from his nearby apartment where he is eating dinner, telephones Wendt at Portal Five, fearing something terrible might be happening. Wendt blurts out that the Reichstag is burning. Scranowitz, ignorant of Wendt's previously frustrated at-

Berlin Fire Brigade at the Reichstag doors. The night was frosty

Ludwig Grauert: Under-Secretary of Interior in Prussia

Hermann Göring: Minister of Interior in Prussia

tempts to reach him, yells in rage, 'And you didn't report it to me!' Dropping his receiver, Scranowitz grabs his set of Reichstag keys and sprints across to the Reichstag. His first concern is to open the doors for the firemen who already have begun to arrive. About this time, Douglas Reed, the Berlin correspondent for *The Times* of London, chances to pass near the Reichstag building and later recollected that the cupola of the Reichstag was 'blazing furiously – a beacon which must have been visible for miles.'

Back at the Brandenburg Gate Police Station in the Alexanderplatz, the young man whom Buwert ordered to call for help arrives at 9.15. Gasping for breath, he blurts out, 'Fire has broken out in the Reichstag!' The young Duty Officer, Lieutenant Emil Lateit, a small, trim figure, instantly calls out the watch and, after a moment's confusion, they pile into a police car and drive at breakneck speed toward the burning building. Such is their hurry that they forget to ask the name of the unknown man who sounded the alarm. After warming himself and waiting a short time inside the station, he leaves and is forgotten.

Part of the confusion at the Brandenburg Gate Police Station is due to the fact that they anticipated a different alarm tonight. The Social Democratic Party was scheduled to launch an election rally at the Berlin Sportpalast. The police had orders to close it down, and Lieutenant Lateit was detailed to handle a portion of the expected consequences of that decision. As a result the police car was already waiting in front of the station with its motor running, so by breaking a few speed records it takes only one minute to reach the fire, at 9.17. Once at the scene of the fire, Lateit quickly takes charge. He is told that the Brigade has been called, but he immediately orders Buwert to sound the 'Grand' or 'Fifteenth Stage' alarm which would call in every fire engine in the city of Berlin, over sixty in all. In the mounting commotion, however, Buwert is becoming overloaded with responsibilities, and in the excitement Lateit has also ordered Buwert to stand guard on the ramp in case the arsonist should show his head. If the arsonist should come into view again, Buwert must shoot immediately. Buwert quite naturally feels his primary duty is to remain standing his watch, and he quite forgets to sound the Grand Alarm.

Meanwhile Lateit runs off to gain entrance into the building. He discovers Portal Two is still locked, as is Portal Three, but he finally reaches Portal Five at 9.20, arriving just in

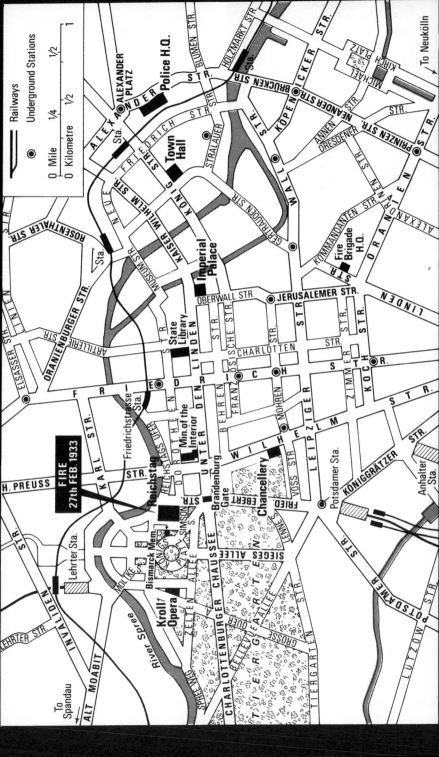

Goebbels: Propaganda wizard

'Putzi' Hanfstaengl

time to meet Scranowitz. Together with Constables Losigkeit and Graening, they enter the burning building; Losigkeit notes that the disbelieving porter still seems astonished at there even being a fire. Once inside, it becomes very dark but nobody turns on the lights. There is a strong odour of burning in the air as they race toward the Restaurant. There they hope to discover some sign of the arsonist or arsonists who have so far remained at large. Upon arrival at the Restaurant they see no one, so they hurry on. At 9.22 Lateit enters the Plenary Sessions Chamber for the first time in his life. Losigkeit and Graening come to his side. Scranowitz remains in the large lobby where he is busy stamping out a small fire near the doorway to the Sessions Chamber while the others are inside the Plenary Hall. Lateit spots a broad wall of flames covering the curtains on both sides behind the Presidential dais. The flames look like 'a burning organ with flames for organ pipes,' he would say later on. He is able to notice little else before turning back. Losigkeit ventures further into the heat and his attention is rivetted by the sight of high, bright red flames rising from the reporters' box to the left and in front of the main dais. Neither Lateit nor Losigkeit see any other flames · in the Sessions Chamber, and Lateit feels certain that

the structure can still be saved.

Coming out of the Parliamentary Chamber, Lateit orders his men to draw their revolvers; he is now convinced that this is a clear case of incendiarism. At this point Constable Poeschel joins them, and Lateit orders him to stay with the House Inspector, Scranowitz. Lateit leaves Graening to continue on his own in the search while he returns to Portal Five with Losigkeit. On the way they pick up a suspicious cloth cap, tie, and bar of soap from the floor of the main lobby. They pass a group of firemen who already have penetrated the building as far as the west lobby. Not knowing that the Sessions Chamber is threatened by a major fire, the firemen busily extinguish minor blazes which they discover cropping up in dozens of places. Lateit sends one of the firemen to the Parliamentary Chamber with Losigkeit. At the entrance Lateit shouts, 'Incendiarism! It's burning to every corner!' Outside, he runs to his police car and then drives at top speed back to the Brandenburg Gate Police Station for reinforcements. He again breaks a few speed records in the process and arrives back at the Station by 9.25, only ten minutes after his original departure. By this time the Sessions Chamber is becoming a roaring inferno. Flames can be seen actually coming out of the

Hitler and Frau Magda Goebbels

cupola by witnesses outside.

Meanwhile Scranowitz finally turns on the lights in the lobby and corridors, accompanied by Constable Poeschel. Everywhere Scranowitz glances he is confronted by flames. He continues dashing about trying to stamp out the smaller fires as best he can. At 9.23, only a minute or so after Lateit and the other policemen had entered into the Sessions Chamber, Scranowitz looks through the door for a few seconds. He quickly takes in the whole scene and sees, as Lateit had, a mass of flames at the end of the room from the floor to the ceiling. He also notices the flames that Losigkeit saw spreading from the reporter's box. But the other things that Scranowitz observes are completely different: small fires all across the far side of the Chamber, on the first three rows of deputies' seats, each about five feet apart and about forty in number. All of these little fires are nearly identical in shape and size, and each is about eighteen inches wide. Poeschel is somewhat behind Scranowitz and cannot see beyond the doorway. Scranowitz slams the door shut and they both run down the southern corridor toward the Bismarck Hall.

Scranowitz is still slightly ahead of Poeschel when they reach the center of the hall. Just then a young, robust, half-naked man, bare to the waist, wearing only trousers and shoes, races across the room from the back

of the Parliamentary Chamber. Scranowitz and Poeschel both roar, 'Hands up!' The apparition is suddenly frozen, his tall body glistening with sweat from the heat. He crouches back in fear and for a moment turns as if to run, but seeing Poeschel's leveled revolver, he meekly surrenders, raising his arms high as ordered. His chest is heaving from exertion, and his long mat of tangled hair is plastered over his damp face. Constable Poeschel rapidly searches the suspect's pockets, discovering a pen knife, wallet, and Dutch passport bearing the man's likeness and his name – Marinus Van der Lubbe. Quivering beside himself in fury, Scranowitz screams, 'Why did you do this?' With a wondering stare at Scranowitz and in a strong foreign accent, the intruder breathlessly puffs, 'Protest! Protest!' Scranowitz, a big burly man with a shaved head and kaiser moustache, is incensed. Scranowitz's fist explodes against the young man's flesh. The time is 9.27. At that moment there is a loud detonation in the Sessions Chamber as the pent-up gasses explode through the glass dome. Seizing his suspect by the naked shoulder, Poeschel wrenches him toward Portal Five. There the prisoner visibly shakes in the cold and a policeman tosses a rug over the young Dutchman's back. By 9.30

19

Marinus Van der Lubbe is in Brandenburg Gate Police Station.

By this time the fire is a virtual sea of flames, leaping upward with incredible ferocity. At 9.31 the Tenth Stage fire alarm is given, automatically calling out two-thirds of Berlin's entire fire-fighting force. Eleven minutes later the decision is taken (for the second time) to give the Grand Alarm, and the city's last remaining fire forces are committed in a desperate bid to save the building. From all parts of the city, over sixty fire engines converge on the burning Reichstag and surround the building. Searchlights are thrown on the walls and in their reflections tons of water pour out through the entrances and flush past the massive crowds that have gathered for the spectacle. Hundreds of policemen arrive by the truckload and on horseback to push the onlookers back to a safe distance. The fireboats on the River Spree are making their contribution felt by sending out seemingly endless streams of river water over the roof on the north side of the Reichstag and into the Plenary Chamber beneath the fractured glass dome. Above everything the blood red flames, billowing

Right: 'Goring's House' adjoining the Reichstag Building
Below: The charred ruins of the Reichstag Restaurant

smoke and steam hiss and snort out of the gargantuan sandstone monstrosity.

About 10.00 Joseph Goebbels is informed of the fire by a call from Ernst Hanfstaengl, a guest of Hermann Göring and who is spending the evening bedridden with a bad cold at Göring's official state residence. Göring, the Speaker of the Reichstag as well as Minister of the Interior in the new Nazi Government, has already left his office at Unter den Linden for the Reichstag. Hanfstaengl can see the flames rising high above the central rotunda of the Reichstag from his room in the Speaker's House, which stands only a short distance from the east side of the Reichstag. Hanfstaengl's telephone call reaches Goebbels at home, where he and his wife Magda are entertaining Hitler. They are listening to records and making light talk after dinner when Goebbels receives Hanfstaengl's message. Goebbels' first reaction is utter disbelief; he refuses to report this 'bit of wild fantasy' to Hitler. Goebbels is convinced that Hanfstaengl is playing one of his frequent miserable bad jokes. Later, however, Goebbels discovers that the fire is real; he had sent his press secretary, Hänke, down to the Reichstag to double-check Hanfstaengl's story, and Hänke came back with confirmation of the news. Goebbels informs Hitler, and they quickly

Hitler in conversation with Prince August-Wilhelm at the entrance to the burning Reichstag

drive to the Reichstag in Hitler's big Mercedes at 80mph, arriving there about 10.30.

Goebbels and Hitler meet Göring, who arrived at 9.35, nearly an hour ahead of them. They all make their way over the jumbled fire hoses and reach the main lobby through Portal Two which Scranowitz has long since opened for the firemen. Within minutes, Franz von Papen, Prince August Wilhelm, and a few ranking civil officials arrive and join the small party of Hitler, Göring, Goebbels, and a half dozen others, who are now looking over the scene of desolation in the Plenary Chamber where the firemen are finally extinguishing the blaze. Hitler seems mesmerized as he stares fixedly at the dying flames from a balcony.

By 10.45 the fire is almost suppressed, although some mopping up will continue until the early morning hours. It has been less than two hours since the first small flame was ignited in the Reichstag. The ramparts are untouched by the fire, and damage to most of the building is slight (except for the pools of water). But the Parliamentary Sessions Chamber is completely gutted as though plucked out from the rest of the building by the voracious flames that had filled the entire room and burst through the glass dome. The iron pillars supporting the broken dome have been convulsively twisted out of shape; they simmer, and the intense red glow slowly fades dead black as if in anticipation of the new era and its colors. Debris lies everywhere, scattered like burned cobwebs. Few witnesses to the scene escape a visceral certainty that Germany has symbolically lost the heart of her parliamentary democracy by an incision worthy of a prehistoric sacrifice to chaos.

The gutted Parliamentary Chamber

In the Beginning...

Until the Reichstag Fire focused attention on the emergence of a new stage in German history, few people genuinely regretted the demise of the Weimar Republic.

In its last years the Weimar regime was rife with plots and counter-plots behind a flaccid façade of bureaucratic functionalism. This impression was particularly profound in the tasteless *nouveau riche* halls of the German Reichstag. The sensation of parliamentary ineptitude was inescapable. No attempt was made to mask the awful din of schismatic bickering on the floor of the Sessions Chamber. Political disorder and inaction had

30th August 1932. The opening of the Reichstag. On the left are the Nazis

become ineluctable companions of Germany's multi-party system. Germans longed for the comparative peace and order of pre-1914 Wilhelmine paternalism; as often happens, their dull recollections were fondly simplistic.

The Weimar Republic had experienced growing prosperity and political satisfaction from 1924 to 1929. Then in 1929 the Great Depression reached Germany from the United States. The bitter anxiety and despair which characterized Germany in the dark years from the 1918 Armistice to the Dawes Plan of 1924 now returned. The German economic collapse worsened from 1929 through 1932. Successive cabinets fell between the two stools of attempting simultaneously to appease foreign powers and reform Germany's internal crisis.

A danger increased that Weimar, unwanted step-child of Germany's 1918 Palace 'Revolution', would die because of its original sin, the Armistice. Crackpots exhorted people to launch counter-revolution and argued that a popular referendum never had been held on the constitution. Most Germans accepted a silly legend that Germany had been stabbed in the back (dolchstoss) at the end of the First World War by conniving traitors. They believed those same traitors and opportunists were responsible for the victory of the enemy and formation of the Weimar Republic. Long processions of unscrupulous fanatics and agitators endlessly repeated these calumnies until the myths were finally accepted wholeheartedly. They pounded home the fact of Germany's weakness vis-à-vis her enemies, the message that even Poland possessed far greater military strength. They tried to inspire a fanatical mass patriotism lacking in the republic. They longed to establish German political and social hegemony over Central Europe. Internally Germans demanded stability. Externally they wanted change. It was impossible to fulfill Germany's needs all at once,

yet people demanded instant solutions. As a result Weimar became inextricably defeatist.

Aching from economic depression, people required over-simple solutions. Perceiving themselves as victims of a Marxian class struggle, they tended to polarise along the mythical co-ordinates required by their illusion of economically determined 'self-interests.' The result intensified existing hostilities and created a reactionary, self-indulgent, and factionalized mass hysteria. Unlike Britain and the United States, the sense of community broke down in Germany during the Great Depression. In social disorientations following 1930, a basic distrust of democracy rotted the soul of the nation. The government of Chancellor Brüning started suspending civil liberties in the name of freedom. Great public scandals surfaced regarding misuse of public funds and abuse of authority. The Weimar Constitution soon represented the ultimate hypocrisy and

chaos of liberty. The civil bureaucracy seemed paralysed by apathy, unable to escape collapse amidst economic landslides. Most Germans disliked the youthful crudeness of National Socialism, but many felt it would fulfill their most urgent individual demands and ambitions. Surely, they said to each other, Nazism could be no worse than Weimar democracy.

At first the army attempted to thwart the success of extremist factions such as the Nazis and the militant branches of the left. But, finally, the army decided to ally itself with the Nazis and the extreme right against all communists and social democrats. Thus, in the aftermath of the Reichstag Fire no attempt was made by the army to halt the violent outbursts of terrorism caused by Nazi brigands.

Parallel to the army another highly developed special interest group played a critical role in the breakdown of the republic. The great landed

Left: 1929 Nazi Party Day in Nuremberg, with Göring, Hitler, and others saluting
Right: Chancellor Heinrich Brüning goes to the polls in 1932

General Kurt von Schleicher, Weimar's last Chancellor before Hitler

Chancellor Franz von Papen in 1932

President Paul von Hindenburg

families of Eastern Germany, the *Junker* class, had performed notable services in the past, but they long since had become conspicuously reactionary. Their dynastic lineages were as carefully protected as their extensive estates. They despised the Weimar Republic while taking, whenever possible, the most fruitful offices in the administration and the army as if that were their natural prerogative. Their rock-ribbed aristocratic pretensions and arch-conservative values grated upon the moderate and socialist parties. Ironically, many ambitious young Germans soon associated the Junkers with the very republic which Junkerdom abhorred. A process of alienation developed and survived until Nazi levelers reduced these imperial fossils to museum-like curiosities. The rise of the Nazi Party owed an indirect debt to the Junkers, however, for these barons possessed none of the resiliency that ought to have contained the Nazis at an early stage. Through combined stupidity, nearsightedness, and immense personal vanity, these uneducated, unsophisticated, yet disciplined aristocrats quietly disappeared like Spanish grandees. They were unloved, and their passing went unmissed. One of the last Junkers to go was President Paul von Hindenberg, but he lived long enough to install Adolf Hitler as chancellor.

German industrialists, too, were just as concerned with pursuing their own self-interests. Yet unlike Junkerdom, German big business was simultaneously political and non-ideological. German industrialists were indifferent to the Weimar Republic, but they cared just as little for a possible restoration of monarchy. Generally preoccupied with expanding their markets and profits, industrialists limited their opposition to Weimar to reforms that directly contradicted their interests. They did not have so much in common with the military and great estate-owners as has usually been assumed. They opposed Weimar's sweeping welfare plans, its intervention in labour relations crises, and its taint of Social Democracy. But most industrialists preferred pragmatism to ideological doctrine.

The contributions of German industry to the Nazi Party equalled only a small percentage of the amount they gave to Hitler's opponents until he became chancellor. There is no basis for the fiction that the industrial cartels financed Hitler's way to power. The fact that the Nazis suffered from a chronic shortage of funds despite tremendous popular support after 1930 indicates that industrial contributions to the Nazi Party had little, if any, effect on the ultimate outcome. Most industrial cliques remained highly skeptical of Hitler until he became chancellor; then they cautiously slipped beside him. Until well into 1933 German business interests failed to gravitate toward a single party. Their leaders until then showed no main party preference for the Catholic Centre Party, the Conservative Party, the Democratic Party, the German People's Party, or the Nationalist Party. This resulted in a diffusion of their political voice, which rarely dominated in any one party.

These characteristics in the mercantile elite were equally true of ordinary German non-Marxists, whether peasants, white-collar workers, or self-employed shopkeepers. Strong internecine political struggles led non-socialist parties into lasting hatred of each other that ignored threats from left and right wing extremists. Unimaginative democratic leaders were completely unsuccessful in establishing a common united front. The divisions never ended between non-socialist factions in pre-Nazi Germany.

Clashing personalities and petty jealousies cut across special interests and determined the outcome of the struggle to master Germany. Just as Chancellor Heinrich Brüning was deposed in May 1932 by Franz von

Papen with the help of President Hindenburg on largely personal grounds, so Papen in his turn was ousted by General Kurt von Schleicher with army support, in November 1932. The process was repeated again with the triumph of the Hitler-Papen team on 30th January 1933. Brüning, Papen, and Schleicher were thoroughly unpopular with the people and the Reichstag; probably ninety per cent of the country was adamantly opposed to Papen and Schleicher. Consequently, they attempted to run the country by presidential fiat without the Reichstag.

The democratic and moderate parties saw their support move towards the Communist Party on the left and the nationalists and Nazis on the right. A coalition was established between the Nazis and communists (and later the Nazis and nationalists). The senile President Hindenburg stumbled into the thicket of reactionary totalitarian suppressions toward which he naturally inclined. He became blind to right wing dissent and reluctant to protect the constitu-

The Fanatics

tion. His contempt for the middle classes, the industrial and banking interests and the socialists differed little from his haughty disdain of Hitler. 'That man for chancellor?' he once said, 'I'll make him a postmaster and he can lick the backside of stamps with my head on them.' Only two special interests mattered to President Hindenburg: the German army and the German landed gentry. And as long as the army and the Junkers leaned toward the National Socialist program, Hindenburg would stray there, too.

Thus, Weimar came to symbolize a short history of failure; its pastiche of decadent sophistication and selfish urbanity became repugnant to German sympathies. Mutual rivalries and animosities at cabinet and party levels left each government drifting aimlessly without either expert or restrained presidential guidance. All that remained for Hitler to do was to develop a logical antithesis to Weimar.

The basic reason for the emergence of a strong totalitarian party in Germany, as elsewhere, was the intense search for a panacea. Hitler

exploited the contradictions and terrors of the masses. With extraordinary skill the National Socialist Party (NSDAP) decisively used the disorientation and consternation following the onslaught of the depression. The National Socialist Party claimed to be revolutionary, but there was a tremendous diversity in their ambitions and theoretical anticipations, a versatility which they retained even after the Reichstag Fire established exclusive Nazi control of the state.

Because of the Nazi Party's diversity, certain organizational principles were needed to provide political maneuverability and cohesion. Compared with the narrow objectives of rival parties, the flexibility of the Nazi Party was startling. Nazism's primary organizational factor was the *Führerprinzip*, or Leadership Principle. This called for absolute dedication, faith, obedience and hope, all directed upward toward the cause as personified solely by one's leader. In return the Leader of Leaders, *Der Führer*, provided action, direction, and protection. One cannot overestimate the importance of this tightly knit hierarchy without which

Nazi Germany never could have existed.

The National Socialist Party molded this formula to contemporary conditions by prescribing it as a remedy for despair and apathy. Touched by a strong apocalyptic vision, Germany had become claustrophobic. The Nazi antidote was to use the *Führerprinzip* for evoking 'The Will to Power', that is, the urge to triumph over the enemy, the need to do Something. This emphasis on incessant activity led each Nazi to accept action without responsibility to any norm but the party and *Der Führer*. Consequently, Hitler provided Germans with the idealized father figure that they had lacked since 1918. The Nazis' acceptance of authority demanded no legal expertise, moral tradition, or administrative rationality. They required more action than thought. In the media of persuasion Hitler's garbled messages were endlessly repeated to proclaim a messianic New Era of The People.

Speaking in Leipzig at the Supreme Court in October 1930, Hitler declared

'How will you vote, Madam?'

'The constitution describes only the arena of the struggle; it does not specify the goal.' The rallying point that Hitler used was principally his claim to represent legality, consensus, order, and transformative redemption. Of course, he pursued this claim by destroying Weimar's rival claim to the same ideals, and in this tactic he had staggering success. His was the only untried answer, and it gathered phenomenal support from large masses of the disillusioned people who felt no readiness to continue a pathetic procession of unsuccessful coalition governments such as had characterized the previous history of Weimar.

Hitler gained his support, at least in part, because of his initial refusal to deal with other parties. This led to a series of spectacular triumphs, because he seemed untainted by their repeated failures. No workable coalition could maintain itself in the Reichstag as elections grew frequent. In 1928 the polls gave Hitler less than a million votes, but that was at the golden height of the republic. Two years later, in the midst of the depression, the National Socialists increased to 6.4 million, rising from ninth place among the parties to second place behind the Nationalist Party. In the March elections of 1932, Hitler's party took advantage of the growing unpopularity of a failing democracy by garnering 11.3 million votes, and by April they rose again to 13.4 million. The landslide seemed inexorable. In July 1932 the Nazis finally obtained 37 per cent of the vote with over 13.7 million ballots to their credit, placing them in undisputed control of the Reichstag. They were the largest party by far; the Social Democratic Party (SDP) reached second place with only about 8 million votes.

But money problems and the unrelenting pace eventually caught up with the Nazi Party. Germany became satiated with Hitler's non-stop campaign; he began to dread the upcoming November elections at the end of 1932. When those final returns were counted, votes for Hitler's party had slightly declined (by two million votes) to

Adolf Hitler on 30th January 1933: Chancellor at last

thirty three per cent despite even larger losses by Social Democrats. The communists meanwhile gained a million votes: an ill omen, thought the Nazis. Hitler was still master of Germany's largest party but he had a gnawing fear that his decline might become as meteoric as his rise.

Thus, Hitler changed tactics and began to cast around for a coalition to win more power, precisely at the same moment that Papen and Hindenburg were seeking some sort of parliamentary compromise between the ultra-right wing of the Nationalist Party and the National Socialist Party. Feeling that he might have little choice, Hitler seized the opportunity and accepted a coalition cabinet. He was installed as chancellor on 30th January 1933, and Papen became vice-chancellor. Two other Nazis and nine nationalists made up the other appointments. Papen and his old crony Hindenburg confidently expected that they would squeeze Hitler into a corner 'until the pip squeaked'. They gleefully congratulated each other on this brilliant coup which had ousted 'dangerous' General Schleicher and, in their delight, they failed to anticipate the disastrous consequences of the following months.

The results of that far-reaching 'compromise' with the Nationalist Party were to provide more freedom of action for the National Socialists and a legitimacy which the NSDAP had never enjoyed previously. The consequences were beyond calculation. With legal authority obtained in the settlement of 30th January the Nazis began making effective use of the largely unexplored resources of the state's civil administration, police services, and armed forces. They gained at one step the necessary patronage which they needed to work out their political will in the war to exterminate the other parties.

Opposition was gradually, and then rapidly, stiffled. When the Reichstag burned the press still had considerable freedom of expression, but by the time of the Fire Trial in September 1933 that freedom had been obliterated by the onrushing Nazi *Gleichshaltung* (the word for imposed 'coordination'). Propaganda was nationally coordinated into a single scheme, and it became a new order in itself, unequalled even by the ferocity of contemporary American political campaign tactics. Radio, press, motion pictures, mass demonstrations – all spoke with a single voice. Hitler was frequently indifferent to the wishes of the average German citizen, yet he knew the paramount importance of establishing mass support for his own leadership. Hitlerite absolutism required the most intimate connection possible with the people and especially with the party. That this first mass age of politics in modern times should be subject to total control from the helmsman was a basic tenet of the *Führerprinzip*.

It cannot be said that Hitler made any attempt to disguise his ultimate dictatorial intentions. He formed no conspiracy, and he set no timetable. He was simply a great improvisor. The electorate in Germany misled itself by believing Hitler's bark would be worse than his bite once he came to power; that had always happened to leaders in their past experience, so it seemed only reasonable to expect the same in the future. Imminent catastrophe even when advertised is rarely recognised. So it proved for Germany in the thirties.

The mystery surrounding the Reichstag Fire was complicated by the sickness of the Communist Party before the fire. This malaise was to be a critical factor in the events following the blaze, when the left wing parties were systematically stamped out by Nazi terrorists. In the last months before the Reichstag Fire neither the SDP nor their hated foes, the communists, dropped their faith and stake in their own ability to survive. Nevertheless, they lost some faith in their ability to unite with other parties in averting the threat of open civil war

Above: A police tactical unit rushes off to stop a bloody fight between Communists and Nazis. *Below:* The Red Banner Front: 60,000 Communists parade in Berlin before 1933. *Right:* Confrontation without honor

So? oder So?

Das neue Jahr – Wegscheide der Zukunft!

Hier Aufstieg und dort Untergang
im Chaos der östlichen Horden!
Hier neues Leben und dort der Drang
nach Anarchie und Morden!

Nur eine Wahl gibt's: So oder so!
Du trägst dein Schicksal in Händen,
Volk, wenn du zögerst, brennt bald lichterloh
Deutschland an allen Enden!

or right wing fascism. This fatalism, particularly after their serious setbacks in July 1932, led to psychological reverses so profound that both the communists and socialists ceased to present effective alternatives to Nazism. They clung to the belief that although the state would collapse they, as individual parties, would survive.

German communists suffered from many of the delusions ailing the Social Democrats but there were important differences. Betrayed by their narrow doctrinal vision, German communists deliberately fostered hatred and suspicion of the other left wing faction, the Social Democratic Party, among the laboring masses, portraying the socialists as revisionist class traitors. The communists delighted in calling the socialists 'Social Fascists', just as they described the Nazis as 'National Fascists'. The communists made every effort to tie German Social Democracy to the imperialism of Versailles and opportunistic bureaucracy. By these efforts the com-

Crowds jeer Nazi demonstrators who dare to march past Karl Liebknecht House, Communist Party HQ in Berlin

munists enjoyed a fair degree of success in undermining the left wing SDP's credibility among workers, but the result turned undecided voters to Nazism rather than communism. Just as the Social Democrats were confident they they could continue functioning under the Nazis because they survived the repressions of Imperial Germany before the First World War, so the Communist Party believed that the Nazis would prove hardly more formidable than the Tsars of Imperial Russia. The Communist Party, by its continued belief that it would be protected by the laws and constitution of the Weimar Republic, was unable to escape the fate of the bourgeois parties. Indeed, since Hitler considered them his greatest threat, the communists were ironically the first to go.

The communist diatribe against the failure of Weimar democracy only immeasurably strengthened the Nazis with whom they had once been allied. Needless to say, the bitterness that the Social Democrats developed as they declined was directed against the communists almost as much as it was against the National Socialists. Con-

sequently, cooperation between the two left wing parties, the communists and the socialists, had become impossible by February and March 1933 when it was direly needed. Neither party had any trust to spare the other.

The German communists and their brothers in Moscow believed that German Fascism was merely the highest, stage of pre-revolutionary and imperialist capitalism. Even today communists frequently suggest that Nazism was initially the tool of German industrialist entrepreneurs, a position that strikes most Western critics as absurd. Since communist ideology tied them to believing that the cataclysm was imminent, no efforts were made to hasten its progress. The communists became complacent as they thought that Marxist prophesies were coming true. Husbanding their limited resources so that they might direct the final triumph of the proletariat in the closing days of the 'battle', the communists watched and waited in anticipation as the Nazi strength grew. Their leaders thought the final stage in Germany's class struggle was unfolding and they had no wish to risk being bitten at this stage in the mad rampages of rabid dogs: better to wait, communist leaders told each other. Thus, despite the Nazi fear of a massive counterattack from the communists during the *Gleichshaltung*, in actuality the left never presented a genuine threat to the new regime. Symptomatic of this malaise was Stalin's renewal of the Russo-German Trade Agreement a month after the Reichstag Fire; there was no major practical reason to renew this agreement at this particular time (it had been permitted to lapse since 1931). Stalin, however, wanted to do everything possible to keep the touchy Nazis at arm's length during what he thought would be the final revolutionary *Gotterdammerung*.

Some German communists were not so sanguine, but they had pitifully little freedom of action. Nazi terror and propaganda worked neatly with communist miscalculation. When the communists belatedly called for a general strike on 30th January 1933, no one came out. In common with the Social Democrats, the Communist Party was bewildered by the superb timing and daring of Nazi success.

By the time Sergeant Buwert fired his shot through the thick glass window of the Reichstag, Germany was ready for the Hitler Reformation. The Nazi *Gleichshaltung* depended upon some sort of explosive provocation, and the Reichstag Fire was the mine with which the walls of German Constitutionalism were breached. As for the German left – or what remained less than a week later – it suffered the fate expressed in Kipling's rueful lines: 'The toad beneath the harrow knows, Exactly where each tooth-point goes.

In fact the Nazi successes were just gaining headway on the eve of the Reichstag Fire. There was an atmosphere of tense excitement throughout Germany, an existential gasp for air before plunging into the fray. The Reichstag Fire put the final seal on the coffin of Germany's leftist parties, but it also opened the way for a revolutionary general assault against all free dissent.

At the same time the Reichstag Fire proved to be a vital and even necessary symbol for launching Hitler's first major and unprecedented step toward political and social amalgamation in Germany. There had been dictatorial practices by the Hitler Government before 28th February, but they were built to the same scale as under the former chancellors Brüning, Schleicher and Papen. The Reichstag Fire, however, marked the beginning of Hitlerite absolutism and the end of German parliamentarism until 1946. The Reichstag Fire was thus a beacon signalling Hitler to smash his foes. But from the shattered debris a few German communists later launched the first international assault against Nazism.

One month to Armageddon

Friday 27th January 1933. Dr Otto Meissner, President Hindenburg's private secretary, dines with the British Ambassador, Sir Horace Rumbold, and expresses his opinions on the current political situation inside Germany. Meissner has long been recognised as Hindenburg's inner voice. He tells Rumbold that General Schleicher, the chancellor, no longer has the confidence of the president. Hindenburg is unwilling to grant Schleicher's demand for a six-month breathing spell before the next election in the event that the Reichstag is dissolved. Hindenburg feels that such a step would be unconstitutional, and Schleicher is expected to resign shortly. Meissner say that a 'majority government' might be formed soon consisting of a coalition that would include all of the right wing parties in a revival of the so-called Harzburg Front. Hitler might become chancellor with Papen as vice-chancellor. Alfred Hugenberg, an ultra-conservative Nationalist Party press lord, might come in as Minister for Economic Affairs. There are signs that Hitler has come to realise that his 'policy of negation' would fail, and that henceforth he would be more moderate. It is expected confidently, according to Meissner, that a Hitler cabinet which included a number of non-National Socialists will prove 'unable to embark on dangerous experiments.'

Meanwhile Chancellor Schleicher hears rumors of a Papen-Nationalist minority cabinet gaining support from the president. Schleicher contemplates using the army to avert civil war in case a right wing coup should pit the Nazis against the government. There is still time to prevent Papen being re-appointed chancellor against the desire of over ninety per cent of the country. Schleicher hopes to prevent the formation of any right wing cabinet, but Meissner, Papen, and Colonel Oskar von Hindenburg (the Old Man's son) effect-

White arm-banded SA auxiliary police

Alfred Hugenberg: German industrialist, press lord, and leader of the German Nationalist Party, who joined Hitler in a coalition cabinet

Dr Meissner and Franz von Papen: the voices behind President Hindenburg

Sir Horace Rumbold, British Ambassador to Berlin

ively shield Hindenburg from all outsiders, who now include General Schleicher. Hurried conferences are held between leading Nazis and Junkers. Hitler has a private meeting with Hugenberg. As plots and counterplots mount, Schleicher manages a last brief audience with Hindenburg, but it comes to nothing.

28th January 1933. Chancellor Schleicher resigns. Schleicher tried to be all things to all men during his fifty-four days in office while hoping to give Germany a strong, moderate government. He detested Hitler, was friendly toward trade unions, and balanced between capitalism and socialism. But he succeeded only in alienating all groups except the army. As John Gunther observed, Schleicher was 'too confident, too ambitious, and too clever by half'.

The Nazis feel that their time is coming. They are wild with delight, and their gangs run amok through the streets. Hitler himself remains cautious, having been rebuffed by Hindenburg before.

29th January 1933. All through the day tension mounts. President Hindenburg still leans heavily in favor of a Papen cabinet, but Meissner and others ask him to consider Hitler as chancellor. At 11pm Papen, Hugenberg and Hitler awaken the president from a sound sleep. He is told that Schleicher is expected to stage an insurrection with army support. Hindenburg is flabbergasted, but his senile mind recalls that Schleicher had said something to him about possibly using force; Hindenburg is now totally confused. Hitler and Hugenberg tell Hindenburg that only by Papen's scheme for a coalition cabinet between the Nazis and the nationalists will civil war be averted. The groggy Hindenburg accepts their plan, gives Hitler the chancellorship, and makes Papen vice-chancellor. The official installation will be made tomorrow. Almost immediately the jubilant new government leaves. Hindenburg falls mercifully back to sleep: the entire episode has only been a bad dream, and things might have been worse. He never has trusted Schleicher!

30th January 1933. General Schleicher goes to work early in the morning only to discover that he no longer has an office. He is aghast. Former Chancellor Brüning murmurs, 'I was treated badly – but poor Schleicher – five times worse!'

The new Government is to be sworn in at 11am. The prospective cabinet assembles in Meissner's study downstairs at the German Chancellery. The members arrive quite awkwardly: several have just learned that it will be a Hitler cabinet, not a Papen cabinet. Everyone is uneasy, and serious disagreements develop over the new government's policy. Finally everyone takes the oath, of office. Crowds gather outside. When the official announcement is made, the country accepts the news with stoic calm.

At 5pm the cabinet meets officially for the first time. The ministers include Franz von Papen, Vice-Chancellor and Minister of Prussia; Konstantin von Neurath, Minister for Foreign Affairs; Lutz Schwerin von Krosigk, Minister of Finance; Alfred Hugenberg, Minister of Economics and Minister of Food and Agriculture; General Werner von Blomberg, Minister of Defence; Captain Hermann Göring, Minister without Portfolio, Commissioner for Air Traffic and Acting Prussian Minister of the Interior; Franz Seldte, Minister of Labor; Wilhelm Frick, Reich Minister of the Interior; and Paul von Eltz-Rübenach, Minister of Transportation and Minister of Postal Services. Of these, only Göring and Frick (aside from the chancellor) are Nazis. The others are all nationalists. With a majority of nine to three, the nationalists under Papen and Hugenberg are confident of their ability to maintain a conservative policy. They have made a special agreement with Hindenburg that Hitler would never be received by the Reich President except when accompanied by Papen. However, the odds they hold will not prove sufficient. Göring, in his role of Prussian Minister of the Interior controlling two-thirds of Germany's administration, is theoretically under Papen's control, as Prussian Minister-President. But Göring will soon exercise absolute authority and ignore Papen. Papen, rather than publicize his ludicrous failure, will put up with Göring's bullying. Papen hopes that Göring will fall on his face, but eventually, people laugh at Papen for a fool: 'He doth nothing but talk of his horse'.

At the first cabinet meeting, Hitler affirms his solemn promise, made earlier to all concerned and particularly to Hugenberg, that new elections will not affect the proportional composition of the present cabinet. He hopes for new elections to give the Nazis enough of a majority to balance the Communist Party influence and perhaps pass an Enabling Act, an emergency law whereby the cabinet may rule without parliamentary authority. This act can only be passed by a two-thirds vote in the Reichstag. Hugenberg suggests Hitler can weed out the communists better by suppressing them than by calling another general election. He believes that suppression of the six million communists will not lead to a strike. The other cabinet ministers are divided on this question. Everyone wants to suppress the communists, but no consensus develops over the means that should be employed. They are all concerned about the danger of doing anything that might precipitate a general strike.

Press response to the Hitler government is mixed. The right wing *Kreuz Zeitung* (Nationalist Party) predicts that the new government will emphasize peace and reconciliation. Because everyone participating in the new cabinet has to compromise both personally and materially, there is every reason to be hopeful that special interests will no longer govern the administration of the country.

The *Völkischer Beobachter* (National Socialist Party) proclaims the birth of a new era. It pays tribute to Hindenburg for the first time and speaks glowingly of the momentous occasion when Hitler and Hindenburg solemnly joined hands.

The moderate *Deutsche Allgemeine Zeitung* sees no cause for enthusiasm. There are great difficulties ahead. Hugenberg is an arch-capitalist. Hitler is an arch-socialist. The Centre Party must demand certain guarantees before accepting the new cabinet. To appoint a chancellor is easy. To remove one is difficult. It is nice to see the new cabinet's efforts to unite diverse sections of the community. But the forces of the left will soon march. Germany will again be divided into little pieces. Her enemies abroad will rejoice.

The *Kölnische Zeitung* (*Völkspartei*) expresses dismay at their exclusion from the cabinet. They are nevertheless thankful that neither Hitler nor Hugenberg has seized control of the vital ministries of Foreign Affairs, Finance, or National Defense. They take courage from the fact that the president still retains the power to prevent any precipitous adventures on the part of the new government. The obvious stalemate between social forces and interests is maintained, and some sort of stability may be inferred.

Germania (Catholic Centre Party) gives the new government an equally jaundiced look. They think that the Hitler cabinet is likely to represent a more parliamentary approach to politics than the authoritarian cabinets of the recent past, but they maintain that the will of the German people has yet to find its true expression. The ironic juxtaposition of Hugenberg and Hitler in the same cabinet is most peculiar. The president and the chancellor are reminded of their constitutional oaths of allegiance.

The oldest newspaper in Berlin, *Vössische Zeitung* (Democratic) criticises Hindenburg for appointing Hitler and warns against the Führer's illegal use of his powers. The newspaper fears

Wilhelm Frick, the Nazi *Reichminister* of the Interior

Baron Konstantin von Neurath, *Reich* Foreign Minister

Meissner, Papen, General von Blomberg, Hitler and Goebbels soon after the Reichstag Fire

29./30. Ausg. · 46. Jahrg. · Einzelpreis 20 Pf. — Berlin, Sonntag/Montag, 29./30. Januar 1933

VÖLKISCHER BEOBACHTER

Herausgeber Adolf Hitler

Kampfblatt der national-sozialistischen Bewegung Großdeutschlands

Unsere Forderung nach Schleichers Sturz:

Kanzlerschaft Hitler

Papens Vermittlungsauftrag mit dem Ziel der Schaffung einer Regierung unter Führung Adolf Hitlers? — Die verweigerte Auflösungsvollmacht

Die Verhandlungen über die Neubildung im Gange

Keine Reichstagssitzung am 31. Januar / Nochmalige Tagung des Ältestenrats

Berlin, 29. Januar

Offene Rotfront-Morddrohung gegen Nationalsozialisten

"Du bist jetzt dran!"

Das Spiel mit der Reichspräsidenten-Krise

Schweres Geschütz gegen Hindenburg

Berlin, 29. Januar

Warum Schleicher stürzte

The Nazi Party press celebrates Hitler's rise to power

Norddeutsche Ausgabe · 31. Ausg. · 46. Jahrg. · Einzelpreis 20 Pf. — Berlin, Dienstag, 31. Januar

VÖLKISCHER BEOBACHTER

Herausgeber Adolf Hitler

Kampfblatt der national-sozialistischen Bewegung Großdeutschlands

Ein historischer Tag:

Erste Maßnahmen der Reichsregierung Hitler

Interview des "Völkischen Beobachters" mit dem Reichsinnenminister Frick — Tagung des neuen Kabinetts

Der Reichspräsident von Hindenburg hat Adolf Hitler zum Reichskanzler ernannt. Der neuen Regierung werden neben Adolf Hitler als Reichskanzler der frühere Minister Pg. Frick als Reichsinnenminister und der Reichstagspräsident Pg. Goering als Reichsminister ohne Geschäftsbereich und Reichskommissar für den Luftverkehr angehören. Pg. Goering wird gleichzeitig mit der Wahrnehmung der Geschäfte des Preußischen Innenministeriums betraut.

Berlin, 30. Januar.

ADOLF HITLER

that if the cabinet falls, the National Socialist leaders may attempt to divert the wrath of the party supporters away from their door and against the Jews.

Vorwärts (Social Democratic Party) perceives that Hitler has finally shown his true colors. The labouring class cannot but fail to see that Hitler is in the lap of the reactionaries. The masses who have supported Hitler must realise that they have been duped. Trade unions must be watchful. If necessary a general strike should be considered; it may be wise to consider a popular front with the communists. Socialist Reichstag deputies will enter a vote of no-confidence against the government. The battle lines are drawn.

The *Rote Fahne* (Communist Party) proclaims a general strike. The issue is seized by the police.

In the evening a grand parade is held honoring the Hitler victory. The president stands on a cold balcony watching 15,000 SS and SA men pass him on their way to salute Hitler. Radio broadcasts throughout Germany proclaim a day of national resurrection. Hitler stands in the window watching until everyone else has gone home. Goebbels writes, 'Everything is like a fairy tale'.

31st January 1933. Hitler and Frick confer with leaders of the Centre Party who, while not represented in the cabinet, must be accommodated in the planning of new elections for a viable government. They agree to a temporary adjournment of the Reichstag but for a shorter period than Hitler wants. Later Hitler decides that he can do without them.

At a cabinet meeting held at 4pm, Hitler obtains cabinet approval of an amended decree 'relating to the restoration of public safety and order' in Prussia. The chancellor later in the meeting promises that the forthcoming election will be the last. 'Any return to the parliamentary system,' he says, 'is to be absolutely avoided'. Papen and the others agree. At the close of the day Papen and Hitler present their proposals for new elections to Hindenburg, who warily gives consent. The country remains uneasy as before, but no organized opposition surfaces.

1st February 1933. Shortly before lunch the cabinet meets again. Hitler expresses fear that a growing popular front has emerged extending from the trade unions to the communists. He declares that the president himself is now willing to abandon to Reichstag. Hitler's chest expands with emotion; the election slogan will be 'Attack against Marxism'! Göring follows Hitler by announcing that terror from the left is increasingly becoming frequent. Special action will soon be necessary to quell the disturbances. Göring doubts that the staff at the Prussian Ministry of the Interior will do his bidding. Upon Frick's suggestion it is decided to hold the elections on 5th March. Meissner, sitting in, says that he will draft the order of dissolution in a manner which will insinuate that Hindenburg has dissolved the Reichstag so that the German nation might express their approval of a 'National Coalition'. Franz Gürtner, nationalist, becomes the Minister of Justice.

The Reichstag is formally dissolved. General Ludendorff, sometime ally of Hitler in 1923, telegrams his wartime colleague, Hindenburg: 'By appointing Hitler Chancellor of the Reich you have handed over our sacred German Fatherland to one of the greatest demagogues of all time. I prophesy to you that this evil man will plunge our Reich into the abyss and will inflict immeasurable woe on our nation. Future generations will curse you in your grave for this action'.

2nd February 1933. In Prussia Göring bans all meetings and political demonstrations by the Communist Party, and a systematic attempt is made to confiscate all communist firearms.

Early in the evening another cabinet session is held. There is a general discussion of a so-called 'Decree for the

Protection of the German Nation'. Papen wishes to add a fine for political insults (to which he is sensitive), and Hitler questions whether it might not be better to stamp out communism after the elections rather than before.

Meanwhile press attacks on the Hitler cabinet continue ever more shrilly. *Vorwärts* screams, 'Out With You'!

3rd February 1933. Göring prohibits the circulation of *Vorwärts* and nearly thirty other Social Democratic papers in Prussia. The ban is to last three days in retaliation for their attacks of the previous day. The communists, however, continue to assault the Social Democrats, engendering considerably increased ill-feeling.

At another cabinet meeting Frick proposes the dissolution of the federal state Diets in Prussia, Saxony, Baden and Brunswick. He suggests that new elections be held there to correspond with the 5th March General Election.

Meanwhile Marinus Van der Lubbe leaves Leiden for Berlin so that he can play his part in the 'imminent' revolution.

4th February 1933. Hindenburg signs into law the 'Decree for the Protection of the German People' which curtails freedom of assembly and of the press. It authorizes the Minister of the Interior and the police to ban public meetings which they deem dangerous to national security, and to censor any publication whether book, newspaper or magazine which is considered detrimental to public order or welfare. It further forbids waging a strike against any vital services. Anyone found in violation of these restrictions, or failing to report such violations, shall be subject to imprisonment.

Konstantin von Neurath, the Nationalist Foreign Minister, smugly tells the British Ambassador that Hitler is a nice man.

Meanwhile the Prussian Diet has come under pressure from the nationalists and the Nazis to dissolve itself while popular feeling is somewhat in their favor. The National Coalition Government needs forty-five votes to win a majority in the Reichstag, but only twelve more seats are necessary to win over the Prussian Diet which controls two-thirds of the land area within Germany. Today the Diet refuses to dissolve.

Goebbels writes in his diary, 'We must take a stronger line with the Jewish gutter press, whose tone is getting more and more insolent'.

5th February 1933. Marinus van der Lubbe crosses the German border on his way to Berlin.

6th February 1933. Hindenburg refuses to act upon the suggestion by Otto von Braun, the Social Democratic Prime Minister of Prussia, that the Reich President refer the status of the Prussian Diet to the Leipzig Supreme Court. Later Hindenburg and Papen proclaim an end to constitutional rule in Prussia and transfer the reins of government there to Papen and his deputies. The decree is called 'For the Restoration of Regulated Governmental Conditions in Prussia'.

7th February 1933. Braun appeals to the Leipzig Supreme Court in an effort to nullify Hindenburg's edict on the grounds that it is unconstitutional. This will be without result.

The Social Democrats hold a mass meeting in Berlin to show their opposition to Hitler's 'reactionaries'.

8th February 1933. *Vorwärts*, reporting on yesterday's demonstrations, chortles, 'Berlin is not Rome. Hitler is not Mussolini. Berlin will never be the capital of a Fascist Reich. Berlin remains Red!'

In a cabinet meeting, Hitler stresses that over the next four to five years the guiding rule shall be 'everything for the armed forces'.

9th February 1933. Goebbels writes in his diary, 'The Jews in editorial offices have become quite humble.'

10th February 1933. Hitler inaugurates the Nazi election campaign in a nation-wide broadcast, which Goebbels terms 'a fine address containing an outspoken declaration of war against Marxism.' Hitler assures the German nation that the National Socialists are harbingers of world peace, national vigor, and cultural salvation. He denounces the Weimar Republic and asks the people, 'Give us four years: then judge us!'

11th February 1933. The newly-formed right wing front, represented by Hugenberg, Papen and Seldte, hold their own election campaign in the Berlin Sportpalast.

Friedrich Stampfer, socialist Reichstag deputy and editor of *Vorwärts*, rejects a proposal by communist labour unionists to wage a united front campaign with the communists against the Nazis. He alleges that the real purpose of such an offer is to divide the social democrats.

Responding to his opposition, Hitler exults, 'Now it is too late for their plans. The time for their ideas is past. No one in the world will help us – only we ourselves!'

12th February 1933. German Catholics are urged by Papen, in an open letter to Hugenberg, to side with the Nazis in promoting a new and more cohesive state. He makes Hindenburg the symbol of the new authority granted to the National Coalition. Hindenburg, however, is known to bear the catholics no love, and the Catholic Centre Party at last proclaims its opposition to National Socialism.

13th February 1933. Goebbels writes, 'Göring is setting things to rights in Prussia with splendid energy. He is the sort of man who does a thing radically, and his nerves are made to stand a hard fight'.

14th February 1933. Göring instructs the Prussian police 'to avoid at all costs anything suggesting hostility to the SA, SS, and Steel Helmet [nationalist 'Veterans Legion'] as these organizations contain the most important constructive national elements'. At the same time he orders them to spare no mercy upon communists and Marxists. He then gives the police open licence to kill all leftists: 'Police officers who make use of firearms in the execution of their duties will, without regard to the consequences of such use, benefit by my protection.'

Von Braun and Severing, Social Democrats – victims of Hitler's wrath

15th February 1933. Major Prussian city police chiefs are replaced by Nazi functionaries upon Göring's orders. Thirteen large Prussian cities are affected, including Berlin. Goebbels clucks, 'Göring is cleaning out the Augean stables'.

Vorwärts is banned for a week along with *Acht-Uhr Abendblatt* and many other well known papers.

16th February 1933. The Catholic Centre Party newspaper *Germania* prints a declaration disclaiming support for the Nazis and urges German catholics to reject dictatorship and extremist views from either the left or the right. This stirring call is taken up by many other papers with a similar political perspective.

The Nationalist Party issues a leaflet proclaiming their 'never-to-be-forgotten battle against the Centre and Marxism'.

The pace of the campaigning is beginning to exhaust the Nazis. Hitler and Goebbels with a few retainers make constant use of the airplane and attend huge rallies all over the country.

17th February 1933. Van der Lubbe arrives in Glindow, outside Potsdam.

The Berlin headquarters of the Communist Party, Karl Liebknecht House, is ransacked by police looking for subversive documents, arms and presses. SA gangs battle with State Party supporters (pro-Weimar) in Oberndorf. Suppression of anti-Nazi newspapers continues on the flimsiest of excuses.

18th February 1933. Van der Lubbe reaches Berlin.

19th February 1933. Göring bans Catholic Centre newspapers throughout Prussia because of the declaration in *Germania* on the 16th. Later this decree is rescinded after Göring yields to pressure from ex-Chancellor Wilhelm Marx, but henceforth the Centre Party will face much more of the Nazi wrath.

20th February 1933. Göring tells Berlin policemen, 'I must hammer it into your heads that the responsibility is mine alone. If you shoot, I also shoot.'

From now until the elections, restrictions on the press will constantly increase.

In the evening Göring invites a number of the most prominent industrial giants to his palace for a little heart-to-heart talk. Hitler is introduced and outlines a number of objectives which he has developed. He vows to destroy the Weimar constitution, the multi-party system, and international appeasement by Germany. He will eliminate Marxism and expand the military establishment. No matter what happens during the elections, the Nazis will maintain control of the country. Göring and Schacht pass the collection box. The big businessmen give in. Well over three million marks are collected. The money is divided between the Nazis, the Nationalists, and the People's Party according to the sizes of their factions in the last Reichstag (a ratio of 196, 52, and 11 respectively).

Stimulated by the fresh funds they have just obtained, the Nazi propaganda machine accelerates its efforts beyond all previous records of intensity.

21st February 1933. Goebbels writes in undisguised glee, 'The rotary presses are thundering and vomiting forth our election materials by the million'.

22nd February 1933. Göring enlists 25,000 SA men, 15,000 SS guards, and 10,000 Steel Helmet ex-servicemen into an active duty police reserve. They are to wear their regular uniforms with the token addition of a white arm band.

Hindenburg is now in despair over what he has done, but he does not know what he should do. Characteristically, he blames Papen.

Sir Horace Rumbold, the British Ambassador, sends London a careful analysis of the German domestic crisis. He notes that the country now resembles two hostile camps which are divided by the Reichswehr and Prussian police. Although the Prussian police are still republican in spirit, their new commanders are doing their best to re-cast them. In the civil disturbances, between forty and fifty people have been killed. Against the minority ruling the country stand a vast majority who embrace every political party except the Nazis and Nationalists. The nation's entire intelligentsia opposes the government almost without exception. German industry, shipping, trade unions, churches, and moderates battle 'a minority composed largely of millions of immature young men and women on whose ignorance unscrupulous demagogues have successfully played.' The Communist Party may be banned altogether, and fears that this will happen may lead many communists to vote socialist instead. On the other hand the difficulties confronting the Social Democrats have been exceedingly discouraging: 'They have an instinct that the dice are loaded against them'.

23rd February 1933. Hitler continues his whirlwind tour of the major German cities by air.

24th February 1934. Frick's threats to southern German states to toe the line or else, result in a major protest to Hitler by the Württemberg Government. Hitler defends Frick in a thinly veiled plea for national unity. Blomberg, the Minister of Defence, calls upon local military commanders to support the Nazis rather than the states in the case of any disturbance during the election period.

The communists hold their last mass demonstration in the Berlin Sportpalast. Ernst Thälmann, the leader of the Communist Party in Germany, makes an impassioned plea for a united front and a general strike with the Social Democrats on communist terms.

A mob of SA men raid Karl Liebknecht House again, led by Berlin police. Göring's men claim to have discovered enormous quantities of subversive documents in clandestine

The Hakenkreuz flies over Karl Liebknecht House on 24th February 1933

Ernest Thälmann, head of the German Communist Party

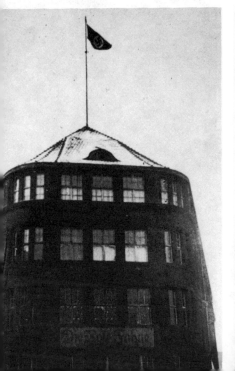

catacombs beneath the communist headquarters. No evidence found in the raid is ever disclosed publicly. This raid will figure heavily in the aftermath of the Reichstag Fire.

25th February 1933. Van der Lubbe sets three public buildings on fire in Berlin: the Neukölln district Welfare Office, the Berlin Town Hall, and the old Imperial Palace. All three fires are seen quickly and doused. He escapes arrest.

26th February 1933. In Goebbels' words, everyone has 'A Sunday's rest'.

27th February 1933. Ernst Thälmann writes an open letter to Social Democratic workers urging them to unite with the communists. A meeting is arranged between Thalmann and two Social Democratic leaders, Friedrich Stampfer and Theodor Neubauer, to take place tomorrow morning. The appointment will not be kept.

In the afternoon a cabinet meeting is held. The Minister of Justice, Franz Gürtner, submits his proposal for a decree dealing with treason against the present government. The Minister of Postal Services and Trans-

Above: Dr Franz Gürtner, Hitler's *Reichminister* of Justice. *Right:* SA troops march through the Brandenburg Gate on the night Hitler became Chancellor

portation notes that the socialists have retained their licence to broadcast the news by radio. He wants to know whether this should be cancelled. Frick and Göring insist that this be done promptly, and tomorrow an order to this effect will be instituted.

In the evening the socialists convene another rally in the Berlin Sportpalast. Friedrich Stampfer is the main speaker. He tells his audience that there exists a profound gulf between a Marxist and an anti-Marxist: 'While the former must have a vast store of knowledge, the latter needs no knowledge at all'. The remark infuriates one of the police officers present who only needed this excuse to close the meeting. The policeman clambers onto the stage and declares the demonstration illegal. The crowd howls in fury, and officials have exceptional difficulty protecting the policeman from being torn to pieces.

At 9.08pm, Marinus Van der Lubbe breaks into the restaurant of the Reichstag and sets the building aflame.

Scapegoat
or Lucifer?

P.D.-Gewerkschaftshaus in München.

Der rote Fuchsbau enthielt: Ge

man, versteckt hinter Kaminen, Maschinengewehre und Handgranaten land...

Rote Gewerkschafts-häuser
und ihre Geheimnisse

Der große Reinigungsprozeß in Deut
Gewerkschaftshäusern nicht vorher
Dokumenti angeblich unpolitischer Bei
stätten marxistischen Klassenkampfes und ei
Deshalb wurden in vielen Städten des
häuser durch S.A. und S.S. ausgehoben
material durchsucht. Die roten Drecßestel
der Hüllung der Hakenkreuzflagge erfolg
deutschbewußten Arbeiter der S.A. und S.
Bei den zahlreichen Durchsuchungen ße
vilproten Bonzen in der Verbergung ihrer
bereitung zum blutigen Bürgerkrieg ihres
wenig nachstanden. Dabei zeigten die tapf
Front" überall das gleiche Bild des Zusam
angesichts der rücksichtslosen Entlarvung ih
ständlich erschienle. Viele dieser verführten
iche Lage unter der roten Herrschaft s
Bürgerbundes gegen ihre Volksgenossen
der Apathie und der Hoffnungslosigkeit,
gewaltigen Strom der deutschen Freiheits
ringliederten.

Auf Lastkraftwagen wird die unermeßli

... seltsame Schlupflöcher ...   ... verborgene Munitionslager ...   ... und seltsame Hintertreppen

From the moment that Constable Helmut Poeschel searched the pockets of Marinus Van der Lubbe, every effort was made to discover who the suspect was, why he was in the Reichstag in the first place, if he was alone, what his political and social background and motives were, and where he had come from. The German

s. die in Schlupfwinkel führen, verborgene Regale mit verbotenen Schriften ...

Die interessanteste Kartothek des Liebknechthauses

Government's labored investigations took two paths: the extremely competent Prussian police investigation to discover 'the truth,' and the remaking of the police findings by the Nazi Party into a tactical political weapon with which to beat the alleged 'communist conspiracy'. The police investigation, remarkable in its thoroughness, was most important for establishing Van der Lubbe's real history and achievement, but the Nazi Party version exerted greater influence upon subsequent political events inside and outside Germany. The discrepancies between these two explanations of the Reichstag Fire created confusion in the courts and in the German press. The international consequences of that confusion cast grave doubts upon the nature of German justice and German due process of law, suspicions which led to widespread acceptance of the communist counter-mythology for over three decades.

On the night of the fire Sefton Delmer, an English correspondent of *The Daily Express*, could count himself the luckiest reporter in Berlin. He was tipped off about the Reichstag Fire shortly after Van der Lubbe was apprehended, and after running an entire mile and a half from his office to the fire (there were no taxis about), he came across Alfred Rosenberg, chief Nazi ideologist and editor of the *Völkischer Beobachter*. Rosenberg was deeply gloomy; he told Delmer, 'I only hope this is not the work of our chaps. It is just the sort of damn silly th¹ng some of them might do!' Delmer noted that this remark 'shows that there was at least one Nazi who had nothing to do with it'.

Later on Delmer was exceptionally fortunate to attach himself to Hitler's entourage with at least tacit permission to survey the scene of the fire with them. There he saw the origination of the official Nazi Party version of the Reichstag Fire. A delirious

Book-burning after the Reichstag Fire

Sefton Delmer, veteran British journalist who overheard the Nazi elite at the scene of the fire

excitement infected the entire group. This was particularly true of Hermann Göring, one of the first Nazis to reach the scene. Both Delmer and another star English reporter, Douglas Reed, witnessed Göring's irate indignation that night and concluded that it was not feigned, and they both accepted Göring's testimony at the Supreme Court in Leipzig months later that, 'It had never occurred to me that the Reichstag might have been deliberately set afire; as I drove up, I thought that the fire had been caused by carelessness, or something of that sort. But when I heard a bystander's casual remark, a veil fell from my eyes. In that moment, I knew that the Communist Party was the culprit.' Such a snap judgment and Göring's extraordinary activity thereafter, were totally in keeping with Göring's style throughout his life. On the night of the fire Göring's eyes gleamed like coals and threatened to pop out of his flushed, bloated face. Delmer recalled, 'He would have loved to have thrown

me out. But Hitler had just said "Evening, Herr Delmer," and that was my ticket of admission.' Göring at once told Hitler that the communists were to blame, and he announced that someone had been caught. Dr Goebbels excitedly asked who it was, but Göring admitted, 'We don't know yet! But we shall squeeze it out of him, have no fear, Doctor!'

Hitler then asked Göring what precautions had been taken, and Göring replied that he had ordered full mobilization of the police, who were protecting every public building in Berlin, just in case. 'We are ready for anything', he said proudly. Delmer was the only outsider to witness this private scene, and he remained absolutely convinced that the Nazis were caught completely by surprise. This belief, coming from a veteran English reporter with a lifetime of experience in Germany, is strong evidence against the theory that the Nazi leaders were behind the burning of the Reichstag.

Soon Vice-Chancellor Papen arrived. Hitler went over to meet him, and grasping Papen's hand in a vigorous handshake, cried, 'This is a God-given signal, Herr Vice-Chancellor! If this fire, as I believe, is the work of the communists, then we must crush out this murder-pest with an iron fist!' Notice that Hitler was not yet sure who was behind the fire. That 'If' is another strong reason for supposing that Hitler knew nothing about the real cause of the fire. At the time Papen felt Hitler merely stated the obvious. After all, a communist had been apprehended at the scene. Recent raids on Karl Liebknecht House had netted communist documents detailing an assassination scheme against government officials (including Papen himself). Göring could be heard telling everyone, 'This is a communist crime against the new government!' Probably the communists had been pushed over the brink into total revolution. Nor was Papen the only one to agree with the Nazis.

The mob outside provided fuel for every rumor (including one false story that police discovered Nazi Brown Shirts loose inside the building). Nevertheless, the aristocratic Papen was repelled by Hitler's intense excitement and thick Bavarian accents. He extracted his hand from Hitler's grip: 'Er . . . Oh, yes. I understand that the Gobelin tapestries have escaped, and that the library most fortunately has not been touched either.' But Hitler was not to be put off by Papen's cold-shoulder: 'We are just about to decide on what measures we should take next, Herr Vice-Chancellor! Won't you join us?' Papen diplomatically declined. He quickly left the scene to report what had happened to President Hindenburg. As Delmer thoughtfully mused, 'Papen must have realised that this fire was just about the end of any restraining power he might have over Hitler, and he was not walking into the lion's den that night'.

Meanwhile the Nazis were asking questions. They asked themselves who might benefit from an attack such as this upon the new regime. The answer came quickly: the communists. They asked the firemen who had done the deed. The answer came quickly: the communists. They asked the police whom had they captured. The answer came quickly: the communists. The Nazis knew how to plan conspiracies and putsches. They thought they could recognise a plot when they saw one. Their conclusions were easily reached: the Reichstag had been fired by the communists in a conspiracy to overthrow the Hitler regime! As Göring explained during the Nuremberg War Crimes Tribunal in 1945, 'You must take into account that at that time the communist activity was extremely strong, that our new government as such was not very secure'.

Everything seemed to fit. What should the Nazis do? In Goebbels' words, 'Now we have to act!' Hitler stood at the balcony looking intently

Dr Alfred Rosenberg, Nazi propagandist and theorist. At first he feared that Nazis might have set the fire

into the flames in the Plenary Chamber far below while the hot gusts of air moved about him. He suddenly turned and screamed: 'Now we will show them! Anyone in our path will be mown down! The German people have been soft too long! Every communist official must be shot! All communist deputies must be hanged tonight! All communist sympathisers must be locked up! And that goes for the Social Democrats, too!' Rudolf Diels, head of the Political Police, turned away in disgust to his adjutant and whispered, 'This is a real madhouse, Schneider'!

The logical repression of the left wing parties following the Reichstag Fire was conducted under an assumption that this was a moment which, in Hitler's phrase, was 'sent from heaven'. But it was also both a rather improvised and a paranoiac reaction to an overt threat. Hasty decisions were taken under the assumption that there was a genuine communist conspiracy. When the ashes began to settle, and it became plain that Van

Rudolf Diels, Chief of the Secret Police

excuses.

'Their knowledge of the building and the staff routine also explains why the police captured no one other than a Dutch communist, who, being a stranger in the building, failed to escape after committing the crime. The arrested man, who is also known in Holland as extremely radical, has been present continuously at the meetings of the Communist Action Committee, where he was drawn in to carry out the act of incendiarism.

'Furthermore, the apprehended Dutch criminal was observed by three witnesses to be in the company of the communist deputies, Torgler and Koenen, in the corridors of the Reichstag at about eight o'clock. A mistake on the part of these witnesses is out of the question in view of the criminal's appearance.

'Because, furthermore, the Deputies' Entrance to the Reichstag is locked at 8pm, and because the communist deputies, Torgler and Koenen, had requested that their coats and hats be sent to their rooms at around 8.30pm, although they did not leave the Reichstag until 10pm from another door, these two communists are suspected of participating in the crime, because it was between these times that the fire was arranged'.

Göring knew that almost everything in his statement was untrue. In the enthusiastic and fearful rush to take the offensive, he obviously felt that his bluff would shake up the communists. Göring showed no hesitation whatever on the night of the fire; he was a whirlwind of frenzied activity. During the night he declared a state of emergency, he suppressed the communist and social democratic press, he ordered the raiding and closing of all Communist Party premises and the arrest of every communist functionary that the police could lay their hands on.

There was no resistance to these measures. The dawn disclosed a new Germany. The 'communist con-conspiracy' was crushed. The instan-

der Lubbe had acted alone, the National Socialists had succeeded in smashing the left wing parties. The Nazis by then were committed to their unwieldy fictions. Göring had made the mistake of proclaiming in a press release the morning after the fire:

'The official investigation of the grave act of incendiarism in the German Reichstag building reveals that the incendiary material could not have been brought inside by less than seven persons, while the distribution and simultaneous ignition of the various fires in the huge building must have required at least ten persons.

'There can be no doubt that because the arsonists possessed complete knowledge of all the rooms in the vast building, they must have had unrestricted access within the house for many years. Therefore there are grave suspicions that the criminals were deputies of the Communist Party, who have been meeting in the Reichstag recently under all kinds of

taneous Nazi counter-blow was vindicated by its results. Election day was now just around the corner, so maximum advantage would be extracted from the fire. There was no time to listen to the babbling Van der Lubbe. He was unimportant. He was only a symbol. The thought for the day was 'Revolution'. Act now. Regard the consequences later. That was the Nazi way.

Hitler gloated to Sefton Delmer, a week after the fire, 'My dear Delmer, I need no Saint Bartholomew's Night. By the decrees issued legally we have set up tribunals which will try the enemies of the state legally, and deal with them in a way which will put an end to these conspiracies.'

The police labored under a different burden. With impeccable Prussian logic, they wanted to know the truth about Van der Lubbe. But how reliable were the police?

After 30th January 1933 the police were under great pressure to transform themselves from the relatively enlightened status they enjoyed in the Weimar Government to an absolute obedience to National Socialism. To some extent they cooperated in these changes, but they refused to act without thinking. They felt a great relief when something akin to peace was restored in the streets after the enormous confrontations of the last few years. Soon, they hoped, they might be able to get on with their primary function of maintaining public harmony. As the first head of the Political Police, Rudolf Diels, recalled many years later: 'Order and Authority! The police knew the effect of those magic words!' The police were still essentially non-partisan, although during the Weimar Republic the police tended to support any legal government of the day. This tendency was not as sinister as hindsight might suppose. Political Police had been formed in extreme necessity under the guidance of the Social Democratic Police President, Carl Severing, a man thoroughly devoted to the princ-

Carl Severing, Chief of Prussian Police

iples of the Weimar Constitution in spirit and practice. He moulded them into an effective and benign – if somewhat hamhanded – guardian of the republic.

The Political Police hated the advance of Nazism and communism, condemning both movements as extremist and anathema to the existence of the republic: 'the Trojan horse in the undefended fortress', as Diels explained it. Not until long after the Reichstag Fire did the Political Police succumb to the pressure of the new Nazi political overlords. The entire Nazi cause disgusted a majority of police, political or otherwise. In the end, of course, the Political Police, later called the Gestapo, became transformed until they were synonymous with the worst barbaric villanies of the Nazi Party. To borrow a phrase from the late John Gunther, they became the Frankensteins of democracy. Diels summarized the process thus, 'Opposition became Resistance, and Resistance was High

Treason – treason against Hitler.'
Nevertheless, it is important – even if
difficult – to remember that when the
Gestapo interrogated Marinus Van
der Lubbe, they were still genuine
liberals. They never beat him, drugged
him, or inflicted any tortures upon
him. Their fair treatment of the
suspect, in fact, may have contributed
to the importance of understanding
the validity of Van der Lubbe's con-
fession. The story of the police interrogation shows, first, that the police
still impartial when Van der Lubbe
was questioned, and secondly, how
facts were twisted later to suit the
official Nazi version of the crime.

When Van der Lubbe was taken
away from the Reichstag he was
brought to the Brandenburg Gate
Police Station by Lieutenant Lateit.
There Van der Lubbe was interrogated. He admitted setting the fire
by himself. He explained that he had
hoped it would begin a revolution to
overthrow fascistic capitalism in
Germany. He attached no more signi-
ficance to the Reichstag building
than its symbolising for him the
center of state oppression. He chose
the Reichstag because it was big and
situated in a prominent location, but
he had also considered burning the
cathedral. Lateit shrugged his
shoulders: the suspect was clearly
mad.

Next, Van der Lubbe was taken to
the Alexanderplatz Police Headquarters where he was confronted by
Diels and Schneider from the Political
Police. The period of successive
police interrogations had followed
almost immediately after the suspect's arrest and while the blaze was
yet being contained. According to
Diels, Van der Lubbe was still breathing hard, his naked chest smeared
with perspiration, and 'a wild triumph
lay in the burning eyes of his pale,
emaciated young face.' Detective
Lieutenant Helmut Heisig, who had
been alerted by a quick telephone call
from Schneider while Diels and his
party were taking Van der Lubbe

from the Brandenburg Gate Police Station to Alexanderplatz, had prepared the setting for taking the suspect's statement.

There were others present, however, which made the first interrogation at the Alexanderplatz almost a circus. As Heisig later told the Supreme Court in Leipzig, 'The whole room was teeming with people. First of all there were the officers from my own and from nearby offices. Then there were Police President von Levetzow, the Vice-President, *Ministerialrat* Diels, *Ministerialdirektor* Daluege, together with a number of gentlemen from all sorts of ministries. Altogether some forty to fifty people must have crowded into the little room, for it was completely packed.' Another observer, Hans Bernd Gisevius, a member of the Gestapo, described the situation in later years

thus: 'All of the bustle and excitement was not very conducive to the progress of the investigation. Van der Lubbe appeared quite pleased with the stir he was causing.' Everyone felt quite free to ask questions, and Van der Lubbe showed no hesitation in answering anyone. Some of those present were anxious to find out whether Van der Lubbe knew of any further plans to set fire to other public buildings or whether there might be other plots that he knew about. These questions wasted time and Heisig eventually became exasperated since he was unable to get on with finding out what had happened. Eventually, of course, the main outlines of the case emerged.

One of the most important determinations made at the very first interrogation was that Van der Lubbe understood German without difficulty, and he was equally capable of expressing himself in quite sophisticated German. Despite a heavy Dutch accent, none of his listeners had

Left: **Marinus Van der Lubbe holds a package of fire lighters** *Below:* **Van der Lubbe's Dutch passport**

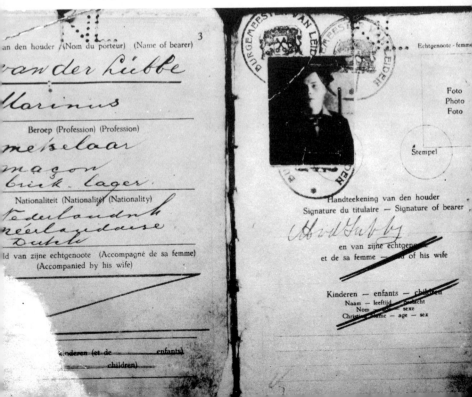

difficulty in understanding Van der Lubbe, who not only talked freely but refused a translator. This was remarked upon in the police report: 'Appearances to the contrary, he is a very bright fellow. His grasp of the German language is so good that he can follow even finger shades of meanings, though his own speech is slurred.'

Hoping to gain additional information, Heisig dashed off a note to the Dutch police in Leyden, the home of Van der Lubbe. The Dutch replied at once: Van der Lubbe was well-known to them. Detective Leiutenant N G Weyers of Leiden reported without hesitation that Van der Lubbe was a communist and considered dangerous.

When dawn came, Van der Lubbe was awakened from sleeping off the night's exhaustion, and further questions were put to him at approximately 8am. A number of curious officials gathered again, but Heisig kept them quiet. This time stenographers took down every word

spoken verbatim. Afterwards, Heisig ordered the secretaries to make as many copies as they could of the transcript, and Van der Lubbe verified the accuracy of every page of each copy with his signature. Detective Lieutenant Walter Zirpins recalled, 'He corrected the statement, going into questions of style and rejecting certain passages out of hand. In short, he had no need of an interpreter.' Van der Lubbe may have been crazy but he certainly was not stupid.

The police reacted to his statements with continued astonishment. They asked Van der Lubbe to retrace his steps through the Reichstag building. He did so without prompting, and he ran ahead of them so quickly that at first they thought he was trying to escape. Heisig later told the Supreme Court: 'We neither indicated the direction nor influenced him in any way. He was almost delighted to show us the path he had taken. He said he had an excellent sense of direction because of his poor eyesight. Another

sense had taken the place of his eyes.'

From the series of interviews and other investigations conducted by the Political Police, a relatively clear picture developed about the suspect, despite the confusing influence of interrogators such as Gisevius who complained because Van der Lubbe stubbornly refused to identify anyone as employing him, or helping in carrying out his arson. The police initially accepted Van der Lubbe's confession. In Van der Lubbe's own words, faithfully recorded by the police stenographers, 'As to the question whether I acted alone, I declare emphatically that this was the case. No one at all helped me, nor did I meet a single person in the Reichstag.'

The police also examined the incendiarist's history to aid them in determing the truth. They found that Van der Lubbe was born in 1909 at Leiden into a life of extreme hardship. He was the son of Franciscus Cornelius Van der Lubbe, a street

Left: Police headquarters on the Alexanderplatz *Above:* Hans Bernd Gisevius, once a member of the Gestapo. After 1945 he blamed the Nazis for the fire

pedlar, and Petronella van Handel-Peuthe, a divorcée who had originally come from a wealthy catholic farming family but separated from them following her first marriage to an important old protestant colonial official. Petronella Van der Lubbe had as little luck in her second marriage, and by the time Marinus was born, she was no longer on speaking terms with his father. Soon the father deserted his wife and children and became a drunken bum. Marinus's mother, who was asthmatic, tried to establish a small shop in Hertogenbosch, the capital of the catholic province of Brabant. She eventually died of exhaustion in 1921, when Marinus was twelve. He was sent off to his half-sister's home where he was treated very well. He became a deeply-religious Calvinist, and the missionary zeal with which he attempted to convert his friends became one of his lasting characteristics.

When Marinus was sixteen years old he was apprenticed by his brother-in-law to a mason. As a bricklayer Van der Lubbe became accustomed to extremely hard work, and his physical skill and agility were so remarkable that his workmates nicknamed him 'Dempsey'.

About this time he was first introduced to Marxism and communism, and communism particularly appealed to his missionary outlook. He was soon reading rather ponderous books which he borrowed from the Leiden Public Library. Slowly, he converted to a crude type of communism cut to the rough lengths of his experience.

Then one day a terrible practical joke was played on him by two of his cavorting friends at lunch. They snuck behind him and pulled a cement sack over his head. Lime dust got into one eye. An operation, however, partially cured him by transplanting mucous membrane from his mouth to his eye. Not long after, his other eye also became damaged by lime when an entire bucket of cement accidentally splashed over his face. He became half-blind for life, despite three more operations. As a result, he could no longer continue his trade, and he went on the Dutch dole, getting seven guilders each week. In his despair he first contemplated suicide, then turned all his energies to politics. The Young Communist League meanwhile welcomed him with open arms, and his dedication to the cause became remarkable. Since his welfare handout was insufficient to live upon, he took a number of menial jobs which often involved heavy physical labour, but his association with communists soon involved him with the police.

Van der Lubbe possessed great native intelligence, and he became well known as a speaker and organizing chairman at the Communist Party. At nineteen he was already permitted to conduct meetings in Leiden and other cities. In addition he wrote a number of pamphlets attacking militarism and capitalism. In 1929, at the age of twenty, Van der Lubbe even rented an empty warehouse which he called 'Lenin House', and presented it to the Communist Youth League for their meetings. He led countless demonstrations, strikes, and marches. Eventually, his stormy nature led to arguments with other communists, and after some fluctuation at length he left the Communist Party ranks at the age of twenty-two in favor of a small extremist splinter group of anarchists, the Party of International Communists.

Meanwhile, Marinus Van der Lubbe inherited his father's wanderlust. At twenty he began to take long transcontinental jaunts not unlike those taken today by college youths. In the late 1920s and early years of the depression, however, behavior of this type was universally frowned upon. This, and Van der Lubbe's membership in a splinter communist group, led the German police into a basic misunderstanding of their suspect's motives. They linked his travels to either a shiftless nature or a means of waging conspiratorial revolutionism. In fact, Van der Lubbe's political associations possessed little international effectiveness, and his travels were motivated by an earnest desire to see a bigger and better part of the world than he had known.

At first he went on brief trips across northern France and Belgium. Then in the spring of 1931 he and a close friend, Hendrik Holverda who was also a member of the Dutch Communist Youth League made plans to travel to Soviet Russia. The adventure's utopian quality appealed to both and at Van der Lubbe's suggestion they poured their energies into earning enough money to make the journey a reality. They printed postcards with their pictures and an inscription in French, Dutch and German, which read: 'Workers' Sports and Study Tour of Marinus Van der Lubbe and H Holverda through Europe and the Soviet Union. Start of tour from Leiden, 14th April 1931.' The gimmick was not original but it made them a considerable amount of money. However, it was not enough to make the journey and, moreover, Van der Lubbe was arrested in Westphalia by Prussian police because he did not have a permit to sell postcards. The result was that Van der Lubbe spent ten days in a Prussian gaol.

Six months later, Van der Lubbe again tried to reach the Soviet Union, this time by way of the Balkans. However his path was deflected by Soviet border patrols, and he ended up spending three weeks in a Polish prison during April 1932 after being arrested for illegally entering the country. He spent three more months in prison after an appeal; he was released in October 1932. By Christmas time he was again in difficulty, not with the law, but with a recurrent eye infection to which he was susceptible after his accidents with lime years before. The disease was diagnosed as tuberculosis of the eye, and he was forced to enter an eye hospital for treatment. He was not released until 28th January 1933, two days before Hitler came to power in Germany.

The news of the new government in Germany stirred the young anarcho-communist to action. After buying every newspaper that he could afford, he became tremendously excited by the prospect of participating in a true revolution. Perhaps, he argued with his friends, this was the moment of the German revolution which would destroy every vestige of capitalist hypocrisy in that country. Van der Lubbe decided that he must go and see what was happening for himself. After a few days' rest, he began the long walk to Berlin on 3rd February 1933. At that time his health was not good: he could barely see, he was weakened from his stay in the eye clinic, and he was suffering from asthma. But he had a stubborn determination to reach Berlin. It was to be his final trip abroad.

By mid-February he neared Berlin. On 17th he stayed the night at a hostel in Glindow near Potsdam. On the next day, Saturday, he hitched a ride by truck into the city of Berlin itself. He wandered from one boarding house to another for the next ten days. During daytime he attended demonstrations held by the Social Democrats and communists. He saw some of these meetings shut down by the police.

In his first few days in Berlin, Van der Lubbe became astonished at the apathy he encountered among the proletarian 'vanguard' of the revolution he had expected. To be sure, many whom he met put their trust in the Communist Party, but no one seemed interested in doing anything immediately to fight the Nazi overlords. Van der Lubbe told his police captors after the fire, 'What the [German] workers' organizations are doing is not likely to rouse the workers to the struggle for freedom. That is why I discussed better ways and means with the workers'.

So Van der Lubbe tried to incite those workers he met into launching at least a few mass protests. But the people to whom he spoke were not interested: they grinned stupidly, nodded incomprehendingly, or slunk off as quickly as they could. They were afraid of him for the most part since he might have been an *agent provocateur* for the Nazis, and the fact that he was obviously a foreigner repelled them. Some told him to take the matter directly to the Communist Party. But Marinus Van der Lubbe, after all, was not a personality to be deflected into the rank-and-file of the Party again. He gradually became desperate to find action.

On Wednesday 22nd February, after wandering aimlessly around the slums of Neukölln, a suburb of Berlin, where he talked to some unemployed workers outside the Welfare Office, Van der Lubbe began to formulate his plans. He came to realise that nobody he talked with was willing to risk his neck for the revolution.

The next day Van der Lubbe attended a communist rally in the Sportpalast. He came prepared to make a speech for which he had made a series of notes. But after arriving and seeing the meeting begin, the assembly was banned by the police, and without serious incident the crowd dispersed. This experience further frustrated Van der Lubbe.

After another day of weary harangues which were met by tired workers' stares or discouraging replies in Neukölln, Van der Lubbe returned to central Berlin in dejection. During the evening he became determined to launch his own individual action on the next day. In his words: 'Since the workers would do nothing, I had to do something by myself. I considered arson a suitable method'.

In mid-morning of the next day, Saturday, Van der Lubbe left his lodgings and headed towards the Neukölln district again, this time with a different intention. On the way he went past Schöneberg Town Hall and the Imperial Palace. He purchased matches at Otto Zöchert's shop in Annenstrasse. Next he went to Brahl's store in Neanderstrasse and bought two packages of 'firelighters', a crude mixture of sawdust and napthalene used to start home coalfires. He requested the brand 'with a red flame' trademark, the 'Oldin' brand. Once outside, he carefully examined his purchase.

Shortly after, Van der Lubbe bought two more packages of firelighters from Heleski's store in Leignitzerstrasse.

At 4pm he headed for the Neukölln Welfare Office, a wooden barracks building which seemed to be the place where workers met together and also a symbol of the social inequities inflicted upon the young Dutchman's entire life. He carefully reconnoitered the building and, since there was still

The Imperial Palace: target for Van der Lubbe's fire-lighters

light, he left the vicinity to return again at dusk.

At around 6.30 Van der Lubbe came back, scaled the fence and lit half of the sticks in one package. These were tossed through an open window which he noticed earlier. They landed harmlessly on the concrete floor of a women's lavatory. Then he threw the remaining half of his open package and half of another package onto the roof which was covered with newly fallen snow. The roof caught fire in spite of the snow, but two people who happened to pass nearby a short while later smelled the fire. They called for a policeman, Sergeant Albrecht, and with the help of a fourth man they extinguished the blaze. The witnesses testified later to the effectiveness of Van der Lubbe's means of incendiarism. Meanwhile, he had long since fled into the city's subway system and caught a train to the Alexanderplatz.

By approximately 7.15pm he arrived

outside the Schöneberg Town Hall. He wanted to set the City Hall on fire because, again, it was 'a building belonging to the system.' He scouted the place and then dropped an entire package into an open basement window of the caretaker's apartment. The occupant, Richard Kiekbusch, was at home sleeping, and at first he did not notice anything unusual. In a very short time the fire burned a large hole through the floor and carpeting, charred a coatrack and singed the wallpaper. Kiekbusch was awakened just in time to extinguish the flames. He reported later in court that 'flammable materials were stored in the adjoining rooms, and the fire might easily have eaten its way through the plasterboard wall into the other flats.'

Van der Lubbe, of course, had not stayed to see what happened. He went on to the grounds of the Imperial Palace. He chose the palace, he told the police later, 'because it lies in the center of the city, and if it goes up the huge flames can be seen from far away.' The pattern was becoming more pronounced.

Shortly before 8pm, in mid-winter darkness, he clambered up a builder's scaffolding on the west front of the building. A few moments later he crept along the edge of the roof to the south side. After searching in vain for something flammable, he finally threw a lighted package of firelighters into a slightly open outer half of a double-glazed window on the sixth floor. The package bounced off the inner window-glass and lay on the sill burning furiously. Another firelighter fell into a ventilation shaft. Almost two hours later, at 10.10pm, one of the fire wardens of the Imperial Palace happened to discover the fire still burning in the windowframe. After running for help, he and another fireman managed to put out the flames with a firehose. The firelighter in the ventilation shaft was also discovered, but it had gone out on the steam pipes. Meanwhile, after setting the window sill ablaze, Van der Lubbe attempted to set fire to a lathe-house atop the Palace roof, but he gave up after the wind blew out the firelighters before they had a chance to burn the wood. By now Van der Lubbe had exhausted his supply of firelighters, so he had to return to his hostel in Alexandrinenstrasse and go to bed.

The following day, Sunday, all shops were closed. Van der Lubbe wandered around to see some sights and while away the time. He walked out as far as Spandau where he watched a Nazi Storm Troop parade late in the morning with some interest. His appearance must have been remarkably haggard because a woman to whom he spoke gave him some food. By later afternoon he travelled on to Henningsdorf and registered with the police as an alien as the law required. The police allowed him to sleep in a small cell for the night.

The next day, Monday, began very early for him. It was 27th February. Van der Lubbe was awakened by the police and he left the station a little after 7am. He and another vagrant who had been in the same cell went across the street where they were each given a cup of coffee without charge. Van der Lubbe began the trek back to Berlin, arriving about noon. He purchased four more packages of firelighters at Hermann Stoll's, 48a Müllerstrasse. After wandering aimlessly, he reached the Reichstag building at around two o'clock in the afternoon.

As he later explained: 'I decided upon the Reichstag as the center of the whole system.' And following his usual procedure he surveyed the building thoroughly. He decided that the west side was the most deserted. A Reichstag official, Richard Schmal, later claimed to have remembered Van der Lubbe loitering about there.

After reconnoitering the building, Van der Lubbe left the area to avoid attracting attention. He ambled through the eastern section of the city. From about 3.30pm to 4pm he warmed himself at the Alexanderplatz Post Office and then read a few political pamphlets he found in the street. Then, fearing that by staying longer he might become conspicuous he departed. Again, he wandered idly around the city. He returned by 9pm to the Reichstag. It was pitch black on the western front of the building. No one was in sight. In preparation he had removed the paper wrapping from the firelighters.

Van der Lubbe mounted the carriageway ramparts on the right hand side of the Grand Entrance. Clutching handholds in the seams of the sandstone wall, he scrambled to the first floor balcony at the front of the restaurant. Crouching in the balcony, he lit a package of firelighters after experiencing some difficulty with the wind. He wanted to light them outside in case he was discovered prematurely.

Finally, Van der Lubbe passed the point of no return. He broke the heavy windowpanes by repeated kicks. The glass was eight millimeters thick. Then he jumped down into the restaurant. He ignited four relatively fair-sized fires using up most of three packages of firelighters. He only had a single package left. He raced to the Kaiser Wilhelm monument in the hall outside, but he could not find anything flammable there. The exertion, emotion and heat were stiffling; he removed his greatcoat, jacket, waistcoat, undershirt and shirt so he was naked from the waist up. Then he put his jacket back on.

He ran back inside the restaurant taking his shirt which he then set on fire to act as a torch. He found a tablecloth in a service room cupboard adjoining the restaurant and he ignited it from his blazing shirt. Stumbling downstairs into the kitchen next, he dropped the flaming tablecloth. The door of the next room was closed, so with a plate he smashed a glass pane in the service hatch. The pieces of the plate were later found. He entered an office though a hall. At that moment he was alarmed by Sergeant Buwert's muffled shot from the carriageway ramp outside.

Van der Lubbe then ran through the deputies' cloakroom and on through other rooms to a lavatory where he grabbed some towels to set afire. Igniting other pieces of cloth that he discovered along his way, Van der Lubbe trailed these burning rags behind him as he sprinted upstairs again and returned to the Kaiser's monument. Ignoring his cap, necktie, and a piece of soap that had fallen from his pocket, he grabbed his coat, waistcoat and undershirt.

By this time Van der Lubbe must have known that he had almost no chance of escaping the building. He ignited his waistcoat and his undershirt, and later his coat, while dashing wildly about setting fires every place he could – plush curtains, wooden panelling, carpets, and even a solid desk went up in flames. At length he entered the Sessions Chamber behind the right side of the speakers' tribune. There he set fire to more draperies and continued darting madly about. Tearing down one curtain to light another, he ran to the top of the Chamber to the Sessions Chamber by the east side, down the corridor, and then dashing up and down a hallway south of that, he continued to light his curtains one after another with amazing abandon. He also set fire to a leather sofa.

Suddenly he heard voices. Startled, he turned and raced out into the Bismark Hall. He found the door locked. He then dropped another firebrand at the southern entrance to the hall and ran back. This was, for him, an unfortunate choice of direction. He ran right across the path of Scranowitz and Poeschel. The incredible escapade was over. He was captured without a struggle.

Everything in the foregoing story of Van der Lubbe's life and crime was revealed during the course of the police investigation, and corroborated by them. Heisig and Zirpins went to exhaustive lengths to double check every possible point in the story. They repeatedly interrogated Van der Lubbe about what streets he had

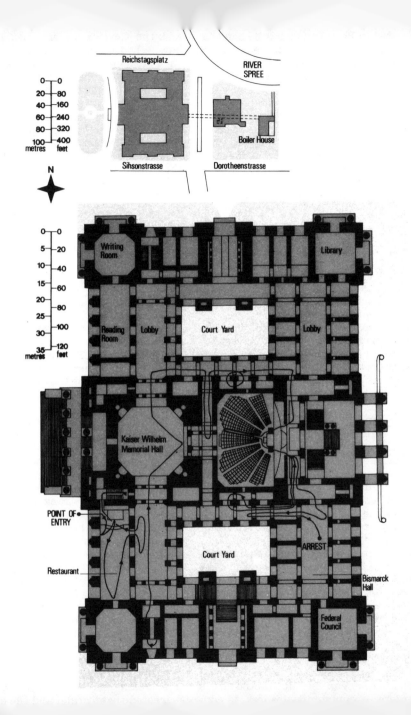

Reichstagsplatz

RIVER SPREE

Boiler House

Sihsonstrasse

Dorotheenstrasse

N

Writing Room

Library

Reading Room

Lobby

Court Yard

Lobby

Kaiser Wilhelm Memorial Hall

POINT OF ENTRY

Restaurant

Court Yard

ARREST

Bismarck Hall

Federal Council

visited in Berlin and what he had seen at what times. Each statement which Van der Lubbe made about his whereabouts was checked and found to match whatever evidence they could find. The same was true of the events in the Reichstag Fire itself. As Zirpins later reported: 'The scene of the crime and his activities there were described by Van der Lubbe right from the start in such detail — seats of fire, damage caused, trails left, and paths taken — as only the incendiarist himself could have supplied . . . The reconstruction of the crime proved that all of the details he gave were absolutely correct'.

The police could not discover a single flaw in Van der Lubbe's story, his descriptions and explanatory drawings. Zirpins concluded: 'There is no doubt that Van der Lubbe committed the crime entirely by himself. This conclusion follows from the investigations, objective facts, and the precise answers of the suspect.' Heisig's opinion was even more explicit. He was quoted at the time and maintained until his death in 1954 that he believed Van der Lubbe caused the Reichstag Fire singlehandedly and had acted solely upon his individual initiative, neither at the instigation of communists nor Nazis. As Heisig reportedly told some Dutch newsmen: 'By treating Van der Lubbe considerately and by letting him feel that he would be deemed innocent until proved otherwise, the German authorities managed to get along with him extremely well'.

The police viewpoint, however, came into a tangle of obfuscating hedgings and contradictory investigations when their version collided with the Nazi Government's will. When Zirpins submitted his final report on 3rd March therefore, he hedged on the question of Van der Lubbe's motive. And he finally wrote instead, 'The strong suspicion that Van der Lubbe acted on the orders of communist leaders, is confirmed by unequivocal facts.' The truth is that Zirpins never proved the slightest connection between Van der Lubbe

and the German Communist Party, but he had to toe the line. After all, the politicians in the Chancellery had already proclaimed, on the morning after the fire of 28th February that 'It has been proved beyond doubt that prominent leaders of the Communist Party were directly connected with the incendiarism.' The government story had to stick at all costs despite the conclusions of the police.

Ridiculous charges were also laid against the most conspicuous communists in sight: Ernst Torgler, the leader of the communist Reichstag faction. Koenen went into hiding and later escaped by leaving the country. Trumped-up evidence was introduced into the files along with some real procedural errors by the police to concoct the myth of a conspiracy behind the fire.

In addition to the statements of the Reichstag employees regarding the late departure of Torgler, Koenen and Anna Rehme from the building on the night of the fire, the Gestapo also 'discovered' two Nazi deputies, Berthold Karwahne and Kurt Frey, who had shown an Austrian Nazi cell leader by the name of Stefan Kroyer through the Reichstag on the same night. These three, instead of reporting to the police, came first to Göring and reported that Torgler had been seen talking to several strangers up in one of the galleries. Karwahne, a renegade communist who had known Torgler for years before joining the Nazis, was familiar with the parlor bolshevism and petite-bourgeois friends that characterized Torgler. Therefore, Torgler's guests that night attracted Karwahne's attention. He described them as slovenly and said one looked like a 'Polish migrant laborer, with truculent expression, a broad, flat nose, and dark piercing eyes'. Karwahne's predictably sordid conclusion was that this cretin was Van der Lubbe. He suggested that Torgler and the others were hatching a plot 'of some kind'.

Göring excitedly sent Karwahne, Frey, and Kroyer down to the

Alexanderplatz police headquarters to tell their story. But there an unthinking police constable made an unforgiveable error in procedure. Before the three Nazis had given the police a physical description of the unknown men whom they had seen with Torgler, the policeman permitted the Nazis to catch sight of Van der Lubbe during the Dutchman's initial interrogation at the Alexanderplatz! Thus the police accidentally allowed their witnesses to draw a conclusion by implication which had not yet been proven. The three Nazis only had to look at Van der Lubbe and then, without the possibility of contradicting themselves, describe him as the stranger whom they had seen with Torgler. Oddly enough, Frey and the Austrian failed to 'identify' Van der Lubbe even then, but Deputy Karwahne succumbed to the temptation: 'That's him!' With this flimsy 'evidence' and under strong pressure from Göring, the police decided to pull Torgler in for questioning. Torgler made their job somewhat easier by reporting into the police station next morning after learning that he was under suspicion. He felt certain that the police would clear up the matter promptly. In the meantime, of course, Göring had already given orders to arrest every communist in Germany. Working from a prepared list of 4,000 names compiled under Göring's predecessor, the Social Democrat Carl Severing, the police and their auxiliary SA and SS helpers carried out Göring's orders. Severing had compiled a comprehensive list of Nazis, too, and Göring reasoned that the list of communists would be equally complete. Once Torgler was in Göring's power, there was little chance that such a convenient scapegoat would be freed.

An unhealthy conspiracy of only two people, however, did not look very formidable. So on 3rd March a reward of 20,000 marks was offered to anyone who would give the police evidence leading to the apprehension of Van der Lubbe's co-conspirators. Pictures

Georgi Dimitrov ten years before the Reichstag fire as a Bulgarian revolutionary

of Van de Lubbe were splashed over newspapers everywhere in the country. There were thousands of false leads as a result of this national appeal. Only one of these trials was of lasting importance, but in the end it proved to be the ruin of the entire 'communist conspiracy' case.

Johannes Helmer, a waiter at the Bayernhof Restaurant on Potsdamerstrasse, remembered a small party of foreigners who came in from time to time and behaved rather suspiciously. They all spoke 'Russian' and dropped their voices whenever anyone approached. Everything about them spelled 'Bolshevism', Helmer thought. Considering that the Bayernhof Restaurant was a notorious Nazi haunt, the waiter thought that the behavior of these strangers was highly irregular. Helmer reported his suspicions, and Detective Walter Holzhäuser showed Helmer a few police photographs on 7th March. Helmer 'recognised' Van der Lubbe; considering that Van der Lubbe's photograph was being plastered all over town, Helmer's feat was not difficult. The detective told

The three Bulgarian co-defendants:
Above: Georgi Dimitrov.*Top Right:* Simon
Popov.*Right:* Vassili Tanev

him to inform the police when the 'Russians' came again. Two days later the waiter did just that. The police responded, and the three men caught in the dragnet turned out to be Bulgarian communists.

They were Georgi Dimitrov, Simon Popov, and Vassili Tanev. Dimitrov and Tanev carried counterfeit passports, but the police had broken a communist counterfeiting ring a few days earlier and quickly recognised the work. A taxi was called, and the police left for the Alexanderplatz headquarters with their prisoners. On the way over Dimitrov attempted to hide a piece of paper behind a seat cushion. Afterward Holzhäuser, who had seen Dimitrov's movement, found a proclamation by the Communist International's executive committee with a date of 3rd March; less than a week after it had been printed in Moscow this piece of paper was in Berlin. It took little intelligence to deduce that the bearer of the proclamation had high contacts in the Comintern. The artful pattern of a conspiracy began to seem slightly more realistic.

The Bulgarians did everything in their power to conceal their identity. But the police worked unceasingly, and eventually their names and past histories were revealed. By incredible good fortune for the new suspects, however, the German police never discovered Dimitrov's real identity in the Communist Party apparatus; if the police had ever found out the truth the Bulgarians never would have escaped Germany alive. Even Torgler did not know the truth until several years later. The amazing fact was that Dimitrov was the European Chief of the Communist Third International, and eventually he became its Secretary-General. Thus, the Bulgarians really were Comintern agents but their presence in Germany had absolutely nothing to do with the Reichstag Fire.

The three Bulgarians were formally charged as co-conspirators together with Torgler and Van der Lubbe in the incendiarism in the Reichstag. The plumbing for the presentation of a legal farce was at last complete.

As has been shown, two main approaches to the Reichstag Fire emerged at the earliest stage. On the one hand the political authorities in power, the Nazis, wished to make the case into an excuse for mass political reprisals against an enemy that they feared above all others: the German Communist Party. On the other hand, the Berlin police were preoccupied solely with trying to apprehend the real culprit or culprits responsible. At a variety of points these two approaches impinged upon each other. In most instances the basic prejudices of the police and their prior experience with political extremist activity inside Berlin during the preceeding decade betrayed their lack of objectivity. To be sure, this was not the case in their second-by-second, inch-by-inch reconstruction of Van der Lubbe's actual history before 1933 or his incendiary activities after arriving in Germany just before the fire. But their lack of objectivity was very conspicuous in the police analysis of Van der Lubbe's inspirations or motives. It was also patent in their apprehension of Torgler and the Bulgarians. As a result of the political abuses to which the police investigations were subjected, the reputation of the Berlin police shattered when the Reichstag Fire case reached the courts. Moreover, impingement between the political and police cases also discredited the Nazis. Because Hitler and Göring were convinced very early (or wished it to be believed) that communists were responsible, they explicitly began to think in terms of a show trial which would disgrace the communists once and for all. Soon the Reichstag Fire Trial would be made to symbolise the Nazi Party's justification for the measures put into effect even before the embers had cooled. The alleged 'conspiracy' proved to be an albatross round their necks, because the clumsy *ex post facto* excuses and accusations simply proved totally inadequate.

The Reformation and the Terror

The fury of the Nazi attack against the enemies of the Third Reich is legendary. The *Manchester Guardian* declared at the time, 'There has never been a more remarkable Fire than that which burned the Reichstag building on 27th February. Whatever its origins, the profits were a huge addition to the Nazi Party poll on 5th March, and besides – what is more important – the beginning of a terrorist campaign against all active critics of the National Socialist Revolution.' One must delve into the barbarism of that period after the Reichstag Fire in order to understand the miserable decline of German jurisprudence that accompanied Marinus Van der Lubbe's last few months of life and the beginnings of international resistance to Nazism. The attack against Weimar institutions and German traditions actually proceeded at two principal levels: the reform or abolition of legal safeguards protecting individuals or groups from physical assault, and secondly, the widespread encouragement by the government of Nazi paramilitary terrorist gangs.

On 28th February Hitler obtained Hindenburg's signature on a 'Reich President's Decree for the Protection of the German People and State.' At one strike a number of articles in the Weimar Constitution were indefinitely suspended. Limitations beyond the normal law were permitted curtailing freedom of the individual, the right of free speech, the freedom of the press, the right of free association with other persons of one's choice, and the right of public assembly. In addition the government was given unprecedented power to read the mail, spy on the telegraph, and wiretap telephone lines. Houses could now be searched without a warrant, property could be confiscated or limited beyond the provisions of the Constitution, and in addition the Reich Government was empowered by the decree to take over the governance

Nazi backlash — political prisoners bound for concentration camps

of any Federal state 'temporarily' for an indefinite period when deemed necessary or in the interests of public order or security. All local authorities in the various Federal states or municipalities were required to carry out all demands made upon them by the Reich Government. Any crime normally punishable by a term of hard labor, including treason, poisoning, arson, explosion, and sabotage, would now be punishable by death.

The decree specifically picked out these crimes because they were supposed to have been planned by communist conspirators. The section on poisoning, for example, was added because Göring proclaimed that evidence collected from raids on Karl Liebknecht House proved that communists planned to poison public water supplies and milk supplies at military and police bases as well as at Storm Trooper and Black Guard barracks. Attempted assassination of high government officials would meet with a capital sentence. Grave breaches of the peace committed by force of arms would be punished in the same way, as would political kidnapping. This presidential decree became the basic law of the land until the Reichstag passed the Enabling Act on 23rd March.

The next great legal step in the national *Gleichshaltung* took place at the 5th March elections. The day before the election was the occasion for the most hysterical Nazi demonstration to date. Goebbels whipped up torchlight marches, mass rallies, and loudspeaker cars. Few if any villages escaped this strident campaign which Goebbels called 'The Day of the Awakening Nation'. It was masterfully executed and left the enemies of the Nazis stunned.

After the frenzied Nazi campaign the German electorate had its last opportunity to go to the polls — and once inside the polling booths they voted almost exactly as they had done in the last election! The results staggered the Nazis who had expected

Der Reichstag in Flammen!

Von Kommunisten in Brand gesteckt!

So würde das ganze Land aussehen, wenn der Kommunismus und die mit ihm verbündete Sozialdemokratie auch nur auf ein paar Monate an die Macht kämen!

Brave Bürger als Geiseln an die Wand gestellt! Den Bauern den roten Hahn aufs Dach gesetzt!

Wie ein Aufschrei muß es durch Deutschland gehen:

Zerstampft den Kommunismus!
Zerschmettert die Sozialdemokratie!

Wählt **Hitler** Liste **1**

A Nazi election leaflet before 5th March accuses the Communists of the Reichstag Fire, and declares that the Communists and Social Democrats plan to set the entire country aflame if they came to power

Reichstagswahl
Wahlkreis Berlin

1	**Nationalsozialistische Deutsche Arbeiter-Partei** (Hitlerbewegung) Hitler — Dr. Frick — Göring — Dr. Goebbels	1 ◯
2	**Sozialdemokratische Partei Deutschlands** Crispien — Aufhäuser — Frau Bohm-Schuch — Litte	2 ◯
3	**Kommunistische Partei Deutschlands** Thälmann — Pieck — Torgler — Vogt	3 ◯
4	**Deutsche Zentrumspartei** Dr. Brüning — Dr. Krone — Schmitt — Bernoth	4 ◯
5	**Kampffront Schwarz-Weiß-Rot** Dr. Hugenberg — Laverrenz — Berndt — Wischnöwski	5 ◯
7	**Deutsche Volkspartei** Dr. Mahler — Dressler — Frau Haß — Müller	7 ◯
8	**Christlich-sozialer Volksdienst** (Evangelische Bewegung) Hartwig — Fräu Ulbrich — Lüthje — Krafeik	8 ◯
9	**Deutsche Staatspartei** Dr. Schreiber — Dr. Clauß — Frau Dr. Edelheim — Machuh	9 ◯
10	**Deutsche Bauernpartei** Dr. Fehr	10 ◯
12	**Deutsch-hannoversche Partei** Meyer — Prelle — Meier — Saller	12 ◯
15	**Sozialistische Kampfgemeinschaft** Fahrenson — Schmitt — Schönborn — Reinhardt	15 ◯

The ballot on 5th March 1933: it was to be Germany's last free election before 1945

to win a solid majority. As it turned out, the Nazis returned a massive number of delegates to the Reichstag, but they still needed pro forma alliance with the Nationalists in order to keep their much-heralded majority government. The Nazis garnered 288 seats with 17.2 million votes representing 43.9 per cent of the vote, a four million ballot increase at the expense of the other right wing and democratic splinter groups.

The left stayed amazingly solid considering the intense barrage launched against it during the entire campaign and especially after the Reichstag Fire. The Social Democrats elected 120 members with 7.1 million votes, remarkably losing only two seats. Their *bete noire* further left, the communists, also proved surprisingly loyal to their party; their supporters showed stubbornness, tenacity and great personal courage by defiantly voting for their party candidates. The Communist Party held on to eighty-one seats and the 4.8 million votes cast represented a net reduction of one-fifth of their position before the Reichstag Fire. The practical value of the communist vote however was nil, since the ban on the Communist Party continued to stand. There was no important defection of voters from the communist standard to the Social Democratic Party; some of the communist losses were of course caused by the reluctance of their more timid supporters to risk physical abuse at the polling places. It was estimated that half of the precincts were guarded by overly curious Brown Shirts and the secrecy of the ballot often became problematical. Nevertheless, the actual number of communists and other voters who stayed away from the polls was quite small; over all almost 90 per cent of the electorate turned out to vote as compared with 80 per cent in the previous election. There were of course communists who defected to the National Socialist Party in this election.

Traditionally moderate political parties had mixed results in this election. The Catholic Centre Party, the only party which had not yet massively opted for or against the Nazis, gained four seats, electing 74 deputies with 4.4 million votes. Their allies, the Bavarian People's Party, lost a seat, returning nineteen representatives. The State Party obtained five seats, and the Würtemburg Party lost half of its meager strength ending up with one deputy. Two other splinter parties, the German Peasant Party and the People's Christian Socialists, suffered small losses, obtaining four and two deputies respectively. The People's Party lost strength to the Nazis and came out with two deputies' seats, a loss of nine.

The most important case was posed by the Nationalist Party, led by Hugenberg and Papen. After an extremely energetic campaign and a strong appeal for their claim as the voice of Hindenburg, they only managed to find 3.1 million supporters, that is, 8 per cent of the total vote with, however, a representation of 52 places in the Reichstag, a net gain of one seat. Their dilemma of power in their alliance with the Nazis was keenly observed by the *Manchester Guardian* thus: 'The Nationalists have little reason to be pleased with their experiences [yet] whatever were the means employed to gain it, the Hitler movement has unequalled popular support in Germany today . . . But the considerations which have turned the Nationalists into "accomplices after the fact" are stronger now than ever. They may bitterly regret their course of action which put Hitler into power. But they are too deeply compromised to turn against the Chancellor. However much they fear and despise the Nazis, they fear the unknown consequences of an open breach still more'.

The continued coalition between Nazis and Nationalists caused the final ruin of German democracy because Hindenburg, the only man with power to stop Hitler, stumbled along behind the bewildered Nationalist coterie. A week after the election Hitler said in his harsh, grating voice, 'Years ago I took up the struggle here, the first part of which may now be considered as ended. A coordination of political life, such as we have never before experienced, has been completed'.

After the elections the radio made an announcement after a long roll of drums that the Reichstag would assemble beside the grave of Frederick the Great in the Garrison Church at Potsdam. The spectacle of the Garrison Church service on 21st March proved one of the most significant stages in the continuing advance of the Nazi onrush to consolidate its newly-won position in the nation. The dignified ceremony reassured the army, chastened the Centre Party, satisfied the Nationalists, and uplifted Hindenburg into ecstasy.

The grand purpose of the occasion was to set the scene and mood for the opening session of the new Reichstag and to still the trepidation of the old reactionaries. The brilliant technique by which this was accomplished was the apparent resurrection of the traditional glories, legends, and traditions of the ancient German kings. On the church floor ranks of the young Nazi deputies sat on the left side facing the decrepit old Centre Party members who were headed by Drs Kaas and Brüning. The Social Democrats were not present. The Nation-

The old and new order. The Garrison Church ceremony in Potsdam

Otto Wels, ageing Social Democratic statesman who led his party in rejecting the Enabling Act in spite of Nazi threats

Dr Ludwigg Kaas, Catholic Center Party leader who spoke in favor of the Enabling Act

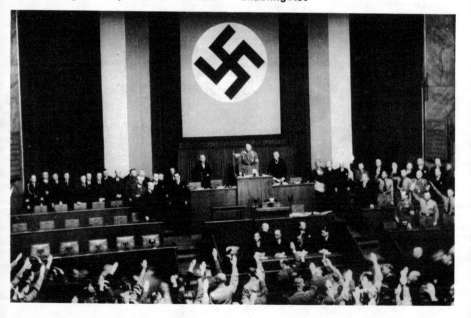

Burnt out of the Reichstag Building, the Reichstag meets for the first time in the Kroll Opera House. Goring presides

alists joined the Nazis, and the smaller opposition parties found places among the Centre Party. In the central gallery rows of marshals, generals, and admirals all dating from the Imperial past sat stiffly in their pre-war uniforms and colors. Below this assembly there was a section of the church which traditionally was reserved for the Imperial family. Here the ex-Crown Prince Rupprecht in full splendor sat behind the vacant Kaiser's seat. Other members of the Imperial family had places behind him.

Hindenburg strode slowly to a chair in front of the Crown Prince. Hitler went to the right hand of the president, and Göring sat on the president's left hand side. The Reich Commissars of the various Federal states were located facing the ministers. The symbolism of the careful arrangements was overwhelming. Then the president invoked the ages past: 'May the old spirit of this celebrated shrine permeate the generation of today, may it liberate us from selfishness and party strife and bring us together in national self-consciousness to bless a proud and free Germany, united in herself'. After an unexceptional speech from the Reich Chancellor, the ceremony ended with the famous handclasp between Hitler and Hindenburg over the grave of Frederick the Great. Outside the church a military procession unequalled since 1914 took place with units from the Storm Troops, the Nationalist *Stahlhelm* veterans, and the Reichswehr taking part. When ex-Chancellor Brüning and Dr Kaas of the Centre Party left, they looked pale as death.

In the afternoon the Reichstag formally assembled for a few hours in the Kroll Opera House nearby. Unhappy critics of the new regime muttered under their breaths that it seemed appropriate to launch the new government upon a theatrical stage. The opening session re-elected Göring as the Reichstag President, appointed its other officers, and gave Göring a chance to deliver a long tirade on the Reichstag Fire and the communist menace.

Two days later, on the morning of 23rd March, the Reichstag reassembled for its first working day. The deputies knew what Hitler expected from them. The Social Democrats present defiantly looked down the gunbarrels of SA and SS squads deployed around the interior of the hall. Machine guns stood in the halls and balconies. The communists, of course, were absent. Reich Minister of the Interior, Wilhelm Frick, had announced a week before, 'The communists will be prevented from participation in the Session by urgent labor elsewhere. In the concentration camps they will be re-educated for productive work. We will know how to render harmless permanently these sub-humans who don't want to be re-educated'.

Hitler entered and gave a prepared speech asking for four years of dictatorship after the Nazi deputies under the control of Göring had succeeded in silencing all opposition. Hitler said, 'The burning of the Reichstag, the abortive attempt to bring a deep-laid plot to fruition is an indication of the fate which awaits all Europe should this devilish doctrine triumph. The real extent of the designs which were to have been carried into effect by this gang has never been fully realised by the German people or by the outside world. A development the catastrophic results of which would have shaken Europe to the roots was averted only by a lightning stroke of your government'.

Hitler ended his speech, asking the Reichstag to pass by a two-thirds vote the proposed Enabling Act, on a threatening note, thus: 'It is up to you. gentlemen! Make the decision now! It will be for peace or war'!

Throughout the speech the Nazi deputies cheered and raved hysterically, knowing their lives depended upon it. From outside the building was heard the tramping boots and chanting chorus of Storm Troopers who demanded, 'We want full powers! If we don't get them, watch out!'

Hitler had set up battalions of Storm Troopers and Black Guards throughout Germany who were to control the entire country if the Reichstag failed to do its 'duty' to *Der Führer*. There was a three hour recess in the Reichstag. The deputies gathered in little knots with grave apprehension written over their faces.

When the Reichstag reconvened, Otto Wels rose to his feet in order to respond to Hitler. The great Social Democratic leader, sixty years old, climbed laborously to the tribune. He knew the mortal danger he invited. His tired body gained strength after a painfully weak beginning, and in a booming voice he repudiated the Nazi Terror: 'We are without weapons, but not without honor!' The other parties turned away a bit sick to their stomachs: Germany had come to this? Hitler, who had been taking notes

SA 'auxiliary policeman' lines up Communists after the Reichstag Fire

feverishly while Wels spoke, then scrambled to his feet in indignation. He viciously ripped into the Socialists: 'Do not take us for bourgeois! The star of Germany is in the ascendant! Yours is about to disappear! Your death knell has struck!'

The deputies cowered under Hitler's wrath. Hitler was followed by Prelate Ludwig Kaas, an expert in canon law and the leader of the Catholic Centre Party. In a deferential voice Dr Kaas declared his party's support for the Enabling Act. The die was cast. Ritter von Lex likewise announced that the Bavarian Peoples' Party would support the Nazis, too. The Nationalists affirmed their support; it was never in doubt. The Enabling Act passed by well over the required two-thirds majority. Göring as President of the Reichstag, announced the results: 441–94. Nobody paid any attention to the fact that it was actually 444 to 94. The Reichstag was in an uproar.

Yet the conclusion had been determined long before. Even if the Com-

munist Party had urged its members to support the Social Democrats in the previous election, it seems likely that the Social Democrats, far from winning the tide, would have been prosecuted at once to the same extent as the communists. As it was, the socialists were outlawed in June. The fact remains, as Papen noted in his apologetic memoirs, the Enabling Act was passed by the Reichstag out of a clear sense by most of those present that it was the only path that might save Germany from civil war. Yet the Nazi threat and their street violence had accomplished that incredible conversion of a democratic to a totalitarian state. Let us now turn to the visceral side of that Terror.

Before the Reichstag Fire a number of villanies had been committed by the Nazis as part of their political campaign, but these in no way compared with the incredible attacks which happened immediately following the Fire. According to an authoritative report in *The Times* (London), appearing on the morning of 28th February, ninety-nine people had been killed in political battles since the beginning of the year. Only a small fraction had been innocent by-standers, however, and *The Times* noted, 'It may be repeated for the sake of proportion that these outbreaks are as yet local, that the everyday life of the average citizen is quite normal, and that residents or visitors see little or nothing of the violent outbursts and suffer no harm or inconvenience from them'. This pattern changed dramatically after the Reichstag Fire.

The ostensible reason for the brutalities which followed the Reichstag Fire was the alleged communist conspiracy, but the Nazis made the event an excuse for practically indiscriminate attacks against all elements in opposition to their political program. Thus they attacked not only the Communist Party but the Social Democratic Party (as 'the communists' next-of-kin'), the Bavarian, Hesse, Wurtenberg, Saxon, and Baden devia-

tionist movements (as 'traitors to the national consolidation of Germany' and 'unsympathetic functionaries'), the Jews (as 'inimical to Germanism and abettors of the proscribed Bolshevik conspiracy'), the independent press (as 'the prostitutes of treachery,' 'the tools of Judah', and 'anti-social hypocrites'), and the foreign press (as 'ignorant dupes of the communist-Jewish propaganda' and 'Germanophobes'). These epithets can all be found in 'coordinated' Nazi press and political pamphlets. To replace the independent voices protesting the Nazi violation of the spirit of the German Constitution, the Nazis relied upon a revolution of systematic intimidation.

The communists, of course, were the first victims of the Hitler terror. Hitler said, 'The fire shows what Germany and Europe have to expect from communism.' And Germany's first concentration camps were specifically formed by the Nazis to contain every communist in the land. Truckloads of SA Storm Troopers and SS Black Guards rolled into hundreds of cities and towns throughout Germany. By the first dawn after the Reichstag Fire, these gangs had arrested hundreds of communists at pistol point. All well-known rendezvous of the communists – even cafes – were closed. The *Hakenkreuz* flag of the Nazi Party was raised over Karl Liebknecht House by the Storm Troopers. Many of the victims were dragged from their beds and beaten in front of their families until they died. Others were taken out into the privacy of the woods and shot in the head. Some were drowned or hacked to pieces with bayonets. The morning after the fire Hitler ranted, 'Our fists will fall still harder and heavier on them'.

Those who were responsible for these crimes were granted immunity even in the few cases where they could be positively identified by the survivors. There was no organised opposition. A few days before the Reichstag Fire, Torgler had summed up the

communist attitude towards the Nazis: 'The Nazis must take power. Then in four weeks the whole working class will be united under the leadership of the Communist Party'. That mentality persisted as the slaughter-house gates yawned. Amid the rubbled ruin of the Communist Party after the fire, the communist rank-and-file were left without direction or initiative. Most German communists were caught in Nazi snares during the first few days. Those who survived the mutilations and the horrors of the SA and SS were thrown into the concentration camps.

The Social Democrats maintained their opposition to the Nazis until they ceased to be important after the Enabling Act was passed in mid-March. But under the repressive new measures the Social Democratic press was completely muffled within the first few days after the fire. During the last preceeding days of the critical 5th March elections, the Social Democrats were harassed by lightening searches of their premises; confiscation of their papers, documents, and files; the imprisonment of some of their most outspoken Reichstag deputies; the suppression of every one of the several hundred Social Democratic newspapers in Germany for two weeks (a week before election day!); murderous assaults by the Nazi goon squads; destruction and seizure of labor union headquarters and meeting places; bans on Social Democratic parades, and proscription of their rallies. In addition the new policy of prohibiting socialist broadcasting over radio stations remained firmly in effect, while the Nazi Party made unprecedented use of the air waves to enormous political effect. The Social Democrats were prohibited from displaying campaign posters, placards, handbills, and pamphlets. They were left with virtually nothing to combat the inspired campaign of the Nazi Party. Under the circumstances, it was amazing that

Burning Synagogue in Berlin in 1933 after the Reichstag fire

the SDP maintained its party support during the elections, losing only 200,000 votes.

The Nazis moved with similar ferocity against protesting Federal states and independent towns. These episodes almost always ended in beatings, whippings, stabbings, huge castor oil doses, and other acts against Hitler's political opponents, whether Centrists, Social Democrats, or non-Nazi local administrators. Sir Horace Rumbold spoke the last word on the subject in a contemporary despatch: 'No Government in this country during the last sixty years has attained to such a position of unchallenged power as the Hitler Government [which] has established a homogeneous authority throughout the Reich, the states, and the communes which Bismark would have envied'.

The Jews, too, were caught unawares by the ferocity of the Nazi onslaught. The Nuremburg Tribunal after the Second World War disclosed no evidence of any concerted or organised physical attacks against the Jews before the Reichstag Fire. But by April 1933 the murder of Jews and the confiscation of their property had become commonplace. The pacifists, communists, and socialists were treated far worse than the Jews at first. When the detention centres were first set up in the days immediately following the Reichstag Fire, there were relatively few Jews there in relation to the other prisoners. But by mid-March when these camps were more established, it was obvious that the Nazi campaign against the Jews would end in raw human tragedy. It is perhaps one of the most despairing facts of life that people often cannot comprehend the probability of their own physical annihilation by their political enemies.

Paranoia is as anti-social as unadulterated hatred, and normal societies reject these extremes. Thus, like many other groups in Germany the Jews had difficulty in imagining a social order malevolent enough to exterminate huge numbers of their people, despite the fact that Jews have known persecution (disguised as prosecution) for thousands of years. The Nazis had made repeated electoral promises to eradicate Judaism from Germany from the moment of their gaining a voice. Hitler wrote in *Mein Kampf*: 'The black-haired Jewish youth lies in wait for hours on end, satanically glaring at and spying on the unsuspicious girl he plans to seduce, adulterating her blood and removing her from the bosom of her own people. . . . The Jews were responsible for bringing Negroes [sic] to the Rhine, with the ultimate idea of bastardising the white race which they hate and thus lowering its cultural and political level so that the Jews might dominate . . . Out of the democratic Jew, the Jew of the People, arises the 'Jew of the Blood', the tyrant of the peoples. In the

course of a few years he endeavors to exterminate all those who represent the national intelligence'.

Goebbels echoed Hitler's debauched babbling: 'The liberation of the German nation can only be carried out against the Jews. It is true that the Jew is also a man. But the flea is also an animal – although not a pleasant one'. Individual atrocities against Jews became more frequent with every passing day after the Reichstag Fire.

The most important fact must not be missed. The Reichstag Fire opened these floodgates of terrorism. The original cause of the hate campaign lay in the murky depths of human despair and animalistic passion. It had chanced to surface in Germany in conditions which are by no means peculiar to that nation alone. The Reichstag Fire began the legitimisation of the Hitlerite terror.

The Nazis also buried Germany's independent press. The basis of that campaign against free expression was

After the fire. Nazis destroy what is 'corrupt' in their national heritage

the Executive Order of 28th February. All communist organs were suppressed at once, and so was the Social Democratic press. But the Nazis did not stop there. The new Nazi press chief, Walther Funk, a remarkably stupid man, told German and foreign correspondents after the fire that he saw no special reason why any papers except those of the Nazi Party should be allowed in Germany after election day. Storm Troopers bullied Catholic Centre newspaper editors into printing Nazi propaganda and censored much of what remained either Catholic or Centrist. The entire democratic press began to ask the 'advice' of ignorant Nazi Party members or sympathisers who 'helped' to determine editorial policy. The newspapers who refused to yield met disaster – their presses smashed, type racks overturned, premises wrecked and then placed under guard. Suppression of their editions for an indefinite period caused many newspapers to fold up insolvent. Moderate and liberal democratic editors, reporters and shop foremen were subjected to sadistic attacks or, if they were lucky, locked up in prisons. Within a short period, the very newspapers which Goebbels contemptuously called 'Jewish press' were too afraid to print stories of the Nazi bloodbath.

The foreign press naturally proved far less willing to accept the dictates of the Nazis, a fact which proved infuriating to the new government. At first the Nazis did nothing against the foreign correspondents in Germany, but even their thick skins quickly became irritated by the continuous stream of 'abuse' from these 'literary assassins' in their parlor. At first the Nazis issued blunt warnings to the foreign correspondents. Later on, some reporters were subject to frightening interrogations by the Gestapo and others were expelled from the country. Individual correspondents lived in terror of 'jumping out of windows in an unguarded moment',

but to their credit they did manage to get the news out of the country – where their home editors tended to whittle it down to something less than inspired accounts. Nevertheless, their first-hand alarm calls against the Nazi terrorism constituted a genuine alternative to the watered-down German versions. As the *Manchester Guardian* said on 8th April: 'The samples of outrages committed by Brown Shirts since the elections make it more evident than ever that the Terror has been much worse than was at first believed. The British, French, and American press, so far from exaggerating it (as the German press complains), has understated the truth, although this is natural enough, seeing that only a small fraction of the truth is accessible . . . All Germany is being converted into a huge prison'.

The Nazi *Gleichshaltung* reached the literary and cultural fields as well. By June 1933 *The Round Table* (London) concluded that despite the authority granted the Hitler Government by the Reichstag, there was no sign of an abatement in the terrorism of the Nazis. Their relentless search to destroy anti-Nazi works and other opposition caused the ransacking of private homes, libraries, booksellers and churches for suspect material. Millions of books were confiscated and ended up in enormous bonfires. Musicians, singers, actors were dismissed from their posts with cultural organisations. German writers, scientists and other intellectuals were harassed, or else saw fit to leave their homeland rather than suffer more persecution. Many other Germans sought refuge in other countries. Hate lists were drawn up against communist, Jewish or anti-Nazi persons and their works. The reformation of the German nation was gradually becoming a repudiation of an intellectual tradition. The *Berliner Lokal-Anzeiger* said on 7th May: 'We are not and do not want to be the land of Goethe and Einstein. Not on any account'.

The preliminary hearing

The Hitler Terror was well under way when the Preliminary Hearing of Marinus Van der Lubbe, Ernst Torgler, and the three Bulgarians began. Under the German legal system, which technically still regarded the rights and privileges of the accused as sacred, a substantial case against the defendants had to be proven in a Preliminary Hearing before the case actually could be tried by the Leipzig Supreme Court, the highest court in the nation.

According to German law, the actual trial of the accused could not take place until after a double Preliminary Investigation. The first investigation was conducted by the police. The police collected all information possible relating to the crime, apprehended the suspects, checked the history of the accused, and indicated their political and social associations. The police findings and evidence were then submitted to the Examining Magistrate. The second investigation, which proceeded concurrently,

was a Preliminary Hearing. It was conducted by the Examining Magistrate, in this case a Superior Court judge.

The objective of this second inquiry was to re-examine the evidence and reports of the police; to question the witnesses who might substantially contribute to the case; to interrogate the suspects; and to present the final report and the indictment to the Public Prosecuting Attorney who would then bind over the defendants for trial. This two-tier system was intended to safeguard the defendants from any abuse in the law, because all evidence pertaining to the crime was sifted by two relatively independent bodies before reaching a court of law for trial. And when a case finally came to trial, evidence revealed in the Preliminary Hearing or police investigation would have to be submitted in direct testimony in open court. Only in the most exceptional circumstances could material presented in the preliminary phases preceding the final trial be used without going through this re-submission procedure.

Thus far the Weimar legal code had been untouched by the Nazi *Gleichshaltung*. Some idea of the thoroughness of the Reichstag Fire Hearing can be gained from the fact that the Hearing, which began in early March, was not concluded until 1st June 1933. Twenty-four massive volumes of testimony and thirty-two bundles of depositions were compiled at the Hearing. Some 500 witnesses were called. The evidence amassed constituted one of the most exhaustive inquiries on a single incident ever known in German history. Yet while the witnesses paraded back and forth, and while the depositions were made, the German Magistrate in charge totally misconstrued the evidence. When he finished his investigations, he bound every one of his five principal suspects over for trial, although it was patently obvious that only Van der Lubbe was guilty.

Because the Reichstag Fire case had to be handed to the Preliminary Hearing to determine whether sufficient grounds existed to try the case in the Supreme Court, Göring took alarm. He was in a unique position to appreciate the general hostility against the Nazis which was felt by most of the German bench. Göring at once voiced his fears to his fellow Ministers at a Cabinet meeting on 2nd March: 'The police will have to turn over the examining of the culprit to the Reich Supreme Court at once. The Examining Judge slated to take the investigation is the Superior Court Judge, Dr Braune, who formerly conducted the examinations of members of the National Socialist Party. He always proceeded most severely against the Party.

'Even if it has to be assumed that he can work objectively, he is hardly a suitable person to handle this important matter. It is possible that he might confine the examination merely to the one that committed the outrage although, in the opinion of the experts concerned, at least six to seven persons must have been involved. He might possibly also release Deputy Torgler prematurely from prison. Inept handling might have intolerable results. Whether another more suitable person might not be entrusted with the investigation of the arson in the Reichstag, which has to be regarded not as such but as high treason, must be considered.'

Hitler responded to this suggestion by remarking that on a previous occasion in 1930 Braune had tried three Nazi Party members of the Reichswehr on charges of high treason. Braune had acted with unbelievable incompetence: 'foreign journalists had made fun of it'. Hitler concluded, 'A judge of greater mental stature must be entrusted with the Preliminary Hearing'.

Unfortunately for the Nazis, the final choice was even more inadequate than Justice Braune. As *The Second Brown Book* observed, 'There are hardly terms strong enough to paint his conduct'.

The choice that the government settled upon was Paul Vogt, a Superior Court Justice. Vogt was delighted to undertake the heavy responsibility and immediately began to conduct his investigation in the unburned part of the empty Reichstag shell for the sake of convenience. Afterward, many observers attributed the Judge's findings and failings to his connivance behind the bench with the Nazis. Lieutenant Heisig, for example, told Franz von Papen at the Allied Labor Camp in Regensburg during 1945 that Vogt's 'chief purpose to ensure himself of a position of influence in the Nazi Party'.

Such an explanation of the motives of the judge is grossly inadequate despite its temptations. Neither the Nuremburg Tribunal nor the Russians (who captured Vogt in 1945) were able to show any connection between Vogt and the Nazis. Vogt's reputation before the trial was fairly good,

Popov and Tanev during their trial at Leipzig

although many of his attitudes seemed quite stern, his attention span short, and his intelligence somewhat wanting. In the words of Fritz Tobias, 'By all accounts Vogt was the very model of a Prussian judge: conservative, correct, unrelenting once he had arrived at a decision, unwilling to temper justice with mercy, and self-assured to the point of arrogance'. The Berlin correspondent of *Neue Zurcher Zeitung* commented, 'His bearing is that of a typical Prussian reserve officer. His legal knowledge and loyalty are beyond question'. Nevertheless, Vogt's chief failing was that he became blinded by his own ultra-conservative prejudices to an extraordinary degree.

Judge Vogt did everything in his power to obtain every shred of evidence connecting the Communist Party, the defendants, the alleged conspiracy, and any other relevant materials. Vast rewards were posted for any information which might bear upon the case. Consequently, hundreds of witnesses came forward, some out of sincerity, but most out of petty greed or because they were the usual sort of crackpots attracted by publicity.

In addition, Vogt invited police chiefs throughout Germany to send him details of communist agitation in their local areas. When the results came in, an analysis of them was compiled and became part of the indictment. The police evidence showed that there was very little communist activity in Germany at that time, but Vogt unhesitatingly continued to maintain the official theory that a grand communist putsch had been narrowly averted by the government's quick response. That theory may have looked good when Vogt first approached the case, but after hearing the testimonies and reading the depositions of hundreds of witnesses, the Judge should have known better when he came to write the indictment. Even though there is no evidence that Vogt was pressured into accepting the government version of the fire, it is remarkable that his conclusion mirrored Göring's off-the-cuff press release issued five hours after the fire started.

Paul Vogt's faults were often carried to unusual extremes. His treatment of prisoners, for example, elicited considerable comment during the case. For five months Vogt ordered the prisoners shackled hand and foot twenty-four hours a day. Recalling this experience in Moscow on the first anniversary of the Reichstag Fire and after being released by the Nazis, Dimitrov described 'The agony of their fetters, the unbearable pain caused by the gashes on their ankles and wrists where the chains cut into them; the sleepless nights which they passed'.

Little Vassili Tanev, who had resisted three days and nights of torture by Bulgarian police earlier in his career, attempted suicide in his cell at Leipzig because of the physical suffering he was undergoing due to his shackles.

Paul Vogt was questioned by Dimitrov during the Supreme Court Trial regarding this style of treatment. Dimitrov read the relevant sections of the German Penal Code which required that prisoners not be kept in chains unless particularly dangerous. Looking up to the President of the Court, Dimitrov cried bitterly, 'I made ten applications, three in writing, to have these chains removed'. Dimitrov turned to Vogt who was in the witness box at the time and said hotly, 'Did you or did you not receive these applications'? Vogt, reddening in the face, was clearly embarassed. The Court President, looking intently at Vogt, asked, 'Did you examine his requests'? Haltingly, Vogt replied, 'I . . . there was no actual application in writing'! Furious, Dimitrov interrupted, 'Three times I made application in writing'! Vogt retracted his earlier statement in a rush, 'Wait a minute! Quite possibly he did. He certainly kept referring to the matter, for at almost every interrogation Dimitrov asked me to remove his shackles. It is also quite possible – yes, I am willing to concede that – he put it in a letter. I cannot possibly remember any more'.

It was not until the Supreme Court President overruled Vogt and ordered the fetters removed that the defendants were granted this right. The Supreme Court demanded a written explanation from Vogt for his reasons for shackling the prisoners. His answer revealed that he had always considered them to be dangerous even though they were not yet proven guilty of the crime. He weakly explained that Van der Lubbe had assaulted an official, Dimitrov had made threatening gestures at Vogt himself, and Tanev had tried to commit suicide. Yet even Vogt realised that Tanev had been driven to that extreme only after he

was chained. The entire issue of the fetters speaks volumes about Vogt's attitude toward the case.

Perhaps the first and certainly one of the most foolhardy mistakes made by Judge Vogt during the course of his Preliminary Hearing was immediately after Lieutenant Heisig contradicted the Nazi version of the Reichstag Fire. Lieutenant Heisig, in the interview he granted to newsmen in Holland on 14th March after making investigations there concerning Van der Lubbe, candidly revealed his opinion regarding the fire. He said, 'As for the important question whether Van der Lubbe had assistants or accomplices, it is probable that he alone started the fire. . .'

Vogt ordered the unfortunate Heisig to return home at once, and Heisig was instructed to issue no more public statements. This would have been only a standard legal procedure to defend the suspects' rights; but in the future it was Judge Vogt who issued communiqués. Then Vogt published a reply in the *Völkischer Beobachter*, the Nazi newspaper, in which he wrote 'A report has been published in a number of papers that Van der Lubbe started the fire in the Reichstag by himself. This is not correct. The judicial investigation has been given good reason to believe that Van der Lubbe did not commit the crime on his own initiative. Details cannot at present be given in the interests of the pending investigation'.

Notice that the investigation which Vogt would conduct had not yet even started when he issued this statement.

Nor was this the only such lapse in point of legal procedure by the Examining Magistrate. On 22nd March, less than two weeks after the arrest of the Bulgarian communists, Vogt issued another premature statement to the press: 'The results of the investigation so far have established that the Dutch Communist incendiarist arrested in the Reichstag at the time of the fire was, during the time immediately before the fire, in touch not only with

German communists but also with foreign communists including some who have been condemned to death or to long terms of penal servitude in connection with the blowing up in 1925 of Sofia Cathedral'. Vogt profited from the fact that testimony during the Preliminary Hearing was supposedly confidential in a trial for treason. He did not even bother to check the validity of the statements of the three witnesses who had given the dubious testimony upon which Vogt based this press release.

The evidence connecting Van der Lubbe with the foreigners came from the unfriendly waiter, Johannes Helmer, who had tipped off the police. Helmer swore in Vogt's Hearing that Van der Lubbe had been present at the Bayernhof Restaurant with the Bulgarians, but if Vogt had shown the slightest imagination, he would have discovered from the police that Van der Lubbe could not possibly have been near Berlin at the dates suggested by Helmer. Furthermore, on the night of the fire Dimitrov himself was in Munich, as an incontrovertible alibi proved.

Judge Vogt's second reason for his public pronouncement came from the engineer Paul Boghun's testimony. *The Second Brown Book* accurately comments: 'The Examining Magistrate seems to have made it his business to assist the witnesses in making their statements. Take Vogt's painstaking treatment of the engineer, Boghun, who asserted having seen a strange man stealing out of the Reichstag at about 9pm on the night of the fire . . . Boghun had originally stated to the police that the stranger was wearing light coloured trousers [but] during his examination by Vogt they darkened perceptibly until they became identical blue trousers which Popov was wearing. Boghun had told the Police Officer Lateit, on the night of the fire, that he could not say whether this stranger was wearing a hat or a cap; but Vogt so charmed his faculty of memory that in the end Boghun was able, even emphatically, to assert that the stranger had worn a soft hat. The Examining Magistrate displayed the same solicitude . . . in attending to all his witnesses.'

The last witness on whom Judge Vogt relied sufficiently to make his public statement was Dr Ernst Dröscher, a press official for the Nazi Party. He informed Vogt that he had recognised a 'wanted' poster in Bulgaria identifying Dimitrov as one of the parties responsible for blowing up the dome of the Cathedral of Nedelia at Sofia in April 1925. Vogt accepted Dröscher's testimony without question. Imagine the Judge's acute embarrassment – and that of the Nazis who made a grand fuss over this 'evidence' – when later in the trial it was proven that Dimitrov had already left Bulgaria when the cathedral was blown up and that the man responsible principally for the crime was one Stefan Dimitrov Todorov, a lawyer, who did not have any connection with or resemblance to Dimitrov. Even the Bulgarian authorities – who bore Dimitrov no love – found Vogt's allegations ludicrous; and the *Manchester Guardian* more seriously charged the Nazis with 'an attempt to hoodwink the world'.

Trying to wriggle out of his predicament when called in as a witness, Vogt told the frowning Leipzig Supreme Court, 'It is correct that a statement was issued to the press which inferred that the three arrested Bulgarians had taken part in the setting on fire or blowing up of Sofia Cathedral. At a later date I stated to Dimitrov that it appeared that this information was incorrect. He himself, however, is responsible for the error, since he failed to correct me when I connected the commencement of the Bulgarian insurrection in 1923 with the outrage in Sofia Cathedral which did not in fact take place until 1925'.

This amazing confusion by the Examining Magistrate did not end there. Three minutes later Vogt reversed himself again by yelling, 'The accused *was* involved in the blowing up of Sofia Cathedral! Yes, Mr Dimitrov! We are a little confused! But you wait awhile . . .'

The courtroom filled with laughter. Dimitrov softly raised his eyes and said, 'I did not ask about Sofia Cathedral. But I asked, and I ask again, about our supposed association with Van der Lubbe. I shall prove that Judge Vogt has conducted the judicial investigation in a biased manner, and that he has deliberately misled public opinion'.

The Court President was furious and told Dimitrov, 'Shut your mouth! I cannot permit you to conduct your defense in this disgraceful manner.'

Dimitrov then asked Vogt if it was not true that his press release had been issued prior to the judicial investigation itself. Vogt, near to tears, replied, 'I had the right to issue this statement! The statement was proved right by the subsequent investigation! We arrested the three Bulgarians only because we could prove they were in contact with Van der Lubbe!'

Vogt's appalling eccentricities did not end there. He also refused to permit the Bulgarians to cross-examine Van der Lubbe, yet according to the Criminal Code this was a right accorded to every defendant.

Instead of first unraveling the facts of the case and then subsequently reconstructing the activities of the defendants up through the actual commission of the crime, Paul Vogt was intent upon finding evidence of any kind which would tend to support his preconceived conclusions. He even attempted to frighten his defendants by interrogating them separately at various times and trying to extract their confessions by telling them that their co-defendants had already confessed. The Criminal Code also prohibited this practice, and this bluff failed completely. Yet instead of reconsidering the case when his attempts failed to elicit any response

Dimitrov at Leipzig

to satisfy the conclusions. Vogt merely became more convinced that his prisoners were hardened criminals who would rather die than tell the truth.

Vogt even admitted publicly that he had never entertained the slightest doubts that the defendants were guilty. Was it not obvious that the defendants were lying? The Judge always answered affirmatively. He stated for example that Van der Lubbe had eventually grown silent or just stubbornly insisted that he alone fired the Reichstag whenever the subject was broached: 'At suggestions that he must have had accomplices he became embarrassed or silent.' The Judge reported, 'I could get nothing definite out of him, and I became convinced that the more I drove it home to him that his statements did not tally with those of the experts, the more determined he became to say nothing'.

Vogt's prejudice put blinkers on his ability to comprehend his own part in Van der Lubbe's growing reluctance to repeat the simple truth. Van der Lubbe had nothing more to say if Vogt refused to believe the truth. After four months of this treatment, it is little wonder that Van der Lubbe obdurately remained silent during most of the trial which followed the Preliminary Hearing. His dejection became increasingly profound. Here he had hoped to set the world on fire, but his judges only refused to believe him. Vogt even testified to the Supreme Court that he thought Van der Lubbe was a 'ready if not an habitual liar.' Vogt said: 'Whenever it was a question of determining whether others had helped him, Van der Lubbe invariably told deliberate lies. He spoke openly only when he explained that he was the big hero who had started the fires by himself'.

Such comments were grist to the international propaganda campaign then being waged against the Nazis. Otto Katz, the great communist agitator and editor of the famous Brown Books, asked his readers why Van der Lubbe fell quiet. He answered his own question by alleging that the Nazis themselves were Van der Lubbe's accomplices. To most observers sitting in the Leipzig courtroom and looking at the apathetic 'half-wit' alternately sulking or laughing, Otto Katz's explanation seemed convincing. Surely a youth as dull as Van der Lubbe was incapable of planning such a spectacular blaze! This impression was reinforced by Van der Lubbe's growing ill-health; the miserable prison conditions made his chronic asthma and eye inflammations unbearable. He sniveled and

Dr Alfons Sack, the Nazi who brilliantly defended Torgler

droolled, hunched pitifully over his chair and played stupidly with his chains like a moron. After a while Van der Lubbe simply blocked the courtroom out of his mind for much of the time while the testimony of other witnesses was given. He went past the point of caring what happened and he fatalistically withdrew into a world of his own, knowing he would be executed in the end no matter what.

Meanwhile, Judge Vogt tried to question Torgler's truthfulness, too. This made Dr Alfons Sack, Torgler's counsel, break out in anger. Sack attacked the Examining Magistrate's deliberate attempts to mislead the defendants. The moment provided one of the most astonishing displays in the proceedings, for once it occurred while Vogt was on the witness stand and was vulnerable to questioning.

Dr Sack: 'Did you attempt to make Van der Lubbe say that Torgler had been involved in the Reichstag Fire by pretending that Torgler had already confessed'?

Vogt (his face reddening in anger, and after a moment of dead silence in the courtroom): 'I thought I might have been spared such a question! I am a German Justice! I am an officer of the Supreme Court! And besides, my name is Vogt, and I believe. . . '

Vogt's voice quavered and he trembled with fury. He buttoned up his dignity as though it were his collar: 'I declare with complete cer-

tainty that I have never ever done anything which was not compatible with the honor of a German Justice!'

The Second Brown Book chortled contemptuously, 'This is perhaps unique among Vogt's statements in that it cannot be contradicted. It furnishes the explanation of the methods which he adopted in the execution of his judicial functions, and it explains his treatment of the evidence and his inhumanity towards his prisoners'.

The Second Brown Book had exaggerated, of course, but Vogt's eccentric behaviour did invite such a harsh judgment on German justice by the watchful world press and historians.

In sum Vogt caused unnecessary delays in the course of justice (even though he failed to pervert it in the end). He undermined the entire case by accepting evidence against the defendants uncritically. He committed serious procedural blunders. He was precipitous. He confused the facts. He was easily flustered by defendants and witnesses alike. He did not pay attention to the progress of the case. All these inadequacies resulted in an ill-conceived indictment against all of the accused.

The indictment was finally signed by Vogt on 24th July 1933. The Third Reich never published it, but considerable parts were revealed during the course of the trial and therefore had an effect upon contemporary opinions of the fire. The German press made much of the fact that it was impressively long. It amounted to 235 pages and had a supplement containing the names of 110 witnesses who would appear for the prosecution. Unfortunately, quantity is not quality.

The indictment was supposed to indicate the directions in which the trial would proceed. It served to charge the suspects formally with the commission of the precise criminal acts. German law required that a properly drawn indictment must show the particular law violated, the speci-

fic deeds and manner in which the defendants each were alleged to have committed the crime, the intent of the accused, and the legal parameters circumscribing the criminality of the alleged acts committed. Vogt's indictment did not meet these criteria, except in the case of Marinus Van der Lubbe. No proper case was brought against Ernst Torgler, Georgi Dimitrov, Vassili Tanev, or Simon Popov, who were instead charged with conspiracy to commit arson. With the exception of Van der Lubbe, none of the defendants was shown to have participated in the actual firing of the Reichstag, or in acquiring incendiary material, or in preparing the premises in advance of the fire. The role of the alleged conspirators was not revealed except through implication or guilty association. It was significant that the indictment stated: 'It has not been possible to establish in what manner the accused individually participated in the commission of the crime charged'.

This indictment presented Dr Karl Werner, the Prosecuting Attorney, with an impossible task in seeing it through the trial. With the meagre substantive evidence at his disposal and a courtroom open to the public, the Public Prosecutor and his staff had no chance to win their case if the court were just. All of the thousands of pages in Judge Vogt's report were tantamount to a negation of the State's case. As Dimitrov wrote to his court-appointed lawyer, Dr Teichert, 'It is most regrettable that the indictment has not been published to this day, for its publication would be my best defence. I am certain that my position, as the accused, is incomparably sounder than that of the Public Prosecutor, who must substantiate his indictment before the court and before public opinion. I don't envy him.'

The closely-knit theory of communist conspiracy from now on would be exposed to the merciless attacks of the world, and it would be found wanting.

The Comintern counterattack

The Communist International was originally caught napping by the Reichstag Fire. Only twelve days before the fire, Karl Radek wrote confidently from Moscow, 'Hitler may be able to destroy the legal organization of the Communist Party. But every blow against it will help to rally the working masses to its support. A Party that received six million votes, deeply linked with the entire history of the German working class, cannot be dismissed from the balance sheet of history. This cannot be done by administrative decrees declaring it illegal; it cannot be done by a bloody terror, or else this terror will have to be directed against the whole working class'.

This muddleheaded thinking continued for months in the central Moscow apparatus of the Comintern. Even at the year's end, *Bolshevik* made the following totally unrealistic appraisal: 'In Germany the proletarian revolution is nearer to realisation than in any other country; and the victory of the proletarian revolution in Germany means victory of proletarian revolution throughout Europe, since capitalist Europe cannot exist if it loses its heart.'

The Reichstag Fire was hailed by Goebbels as *Das Fanal*, the beacon. But the Comintern knew that no orders for a revolution had been given. Nor could the highly disciplined central organisation of the German communists discover evidence of involvement by any other communist groups.

Each side knew that the Reichstag was not their own deliberate arson, so each side assumed that the other was using the fire as a deliberate provocation to overpower the other. The question that communists as well as Nazis posed was *cui bono?* Who benefited? The communists averred that it was the Nazis who stood to benefit most from the fire. Therefore the communists relentlessly developed the whole episode into an international *cause célèbre*, and the world

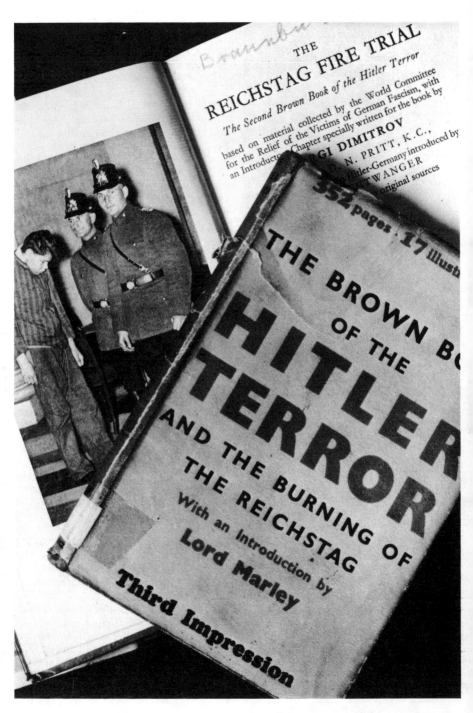

The Brown Book: perhaps the most brilliantly conceived propaganda work of the period between the two World Wars

Karl Radek

believed much of their story.

The communist plan to discredit the Nazis was geared to the Nazi actions after the fire. The two movements developed mirror symmetry with respect to each other. Like the Nazis, the Comintern put to good use every propaganda technique they could find. At first they relied a great deal upon invention and guesswork, since they had no idea of the precise happenings at the Reichstag on the night of the fire. Thus, for example, Göring had said the communists used a tunnel system to escape; equally, the communists said the Nazis had used it. Eventually, the Public Prosecutor proved that no one had used the tunnel.

The stories of some 60,000 German political refugees became staple fare for the communist propaganda machine. Failing to work their revolution inside Germany, communist mass protests were organized abroad. They probably had no alternative. Evidence showed that inside Germany the highly publicized 'communist solidarity' had crumbled at the very first strike of the Nazi sledgehammer. As an eminent authority on the German Communist Party, Ossip K Flechtheim, observed: 'In the course of fourteen years the Party managed to build up an organisation with hundreds of thousands of members, dozens of newspapers, millions of voters, and hundreds of parliamentary deputies. On the day after the Reichstag Fire, all that remained was a little group of harried officials and leaderless fellow-travellers'.

Outside Germany, the communists found ample fuel for a counterattack. After the first shock of Nazi terror, foreign observers turned pale at the news of violence within Germany. Foreign correspondents in Berlin and other large German cities faithfully recorded the onrush of events in the last days before the 5th March elections. Reporters who had seen the fire

HOW WE WON THE AIR WAR IN WORLD WAR II

The story of the B-17s and the men who flew them

CREW MEMBERS OF "ROSIE'S RIVETERS"

FLYING FORTRESS
The Illustrated Biography of the B-17s and the Men Who Flew Them · by EDWARD JABLONSKI

Samuel Eliot Morison

ALBERT SPEER

Take any 4 books for only 98¢

if you join now and agree to accept only
4 selections or alternates during the next two years.

See inside for complete details ▶

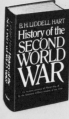

EXTRA FEATURES:
■ Original Blueprint Drawings of the B-17, from wings and fuselage to engines and guns.
■ Pilot's Training Manual—how to fly the B-17.
Even how to ditch it.

B-17 TAIL-GUNNER READY FOR ACTION

FLYING FORTRESS
The illustrated Biography of the B-17s and the Men Who Flew Them · by EDWARD JABLONSKI

8755. **Flying Fortress.** Edward Jablonski. The B-17s and the men who flew them. 400 album photos. Pub. ed. $10.95

The MILITARY BOOK CLUB
Dept. 22-MAP, Garden City, N.Y. 11530

Please accept my application for membership in the Military Book Club and send me the 4 books whose numbers I have printed in the boxes below. Bill me only 98¢, plus shipping and handling, for all 4.

About every 4 weeks, send me the Club's bulletin, **Battles and Leaders,** describing the next Featured Selection and a variety of Alternate choices. If I wish to receive the Featured Selection, I need do nothing; it will be shipped to me automatically. Whenever I prefer an Alternate, or no book at all, I will notify you by the date specified by returning the convenient form always provided.

I need take only 4 Selections or Alternates during the next two years, and may resign any time thereafter. The prices of books offered will average 30% below the prices of publishers' editions, plus a modest charge for shipping and handling.

NO-RISK GUARANTEE: If not delighted, I may return the entire introductory package within 10 days. Membership will be canceled and I will owe nothing.

Mr.
Mrs. _____
Miss   (please print)

Address _____

City _____

State _____ Zip _____

Members accepted in U.S.A. only.

┌─FOR OFFICE USE ONLY─┐

The Military Book Club offers its own complete, hardbound editions, sometimes altered slightly in size to fit special presses and save members even more.

7-M8M

(continued from inside)
book can. Take it, if you wish, as one of your 4 introductory books, along with trial membership.

Look over the books described inside. You won't find a listing like it in any other book club. The MILITARY BOOK CLUB offers you an exciting range of books on hot wars and cold ones. Important combat biographies and revealing memoirs. Significant books on military history and international affairs. Savings are always substantial, too. On the average, 30% below publishers' edition prices, plus shipping and handling.

You're invited to try the Club on a trial-membership basis. Simply choose any 4 books (including, if you wish, *Flying Fortress*). They are worth up to $50 in the original publishers' editions. Take them all

B-17 s CROSSING THE ENGLISH CHANNEL
U.S. AIR FORCE PHOTOS

for only 98¢, plus shipping and handling. But send no money now. Examine the books for 10 days without charge and keep them only if you're delighted.

The Military Book Club
Garden City, N.Y. 11530

quickly grew skeptical of the truth of Government communiqués regarding a 'communist conspiracy'. Within three days the foreign press corps in Berlin began sending questioning articles to their home editors. As the puzzlement of Western journalists found expression in the leading international papers, Goebbels and Hitler became furious. As the *New York Times* reported, 'Nothing so riles any Nazi as reading that some papers abroad decline to hold communists solely responsible for the Reichstag blaze'.

Thus, a natural avenue opened for communist retaliation, and two men outside Germany played a critical role in formulating the Comintern attacks. The first was Willi Münzenberg, a brilliant young professional communist. He was known during happier days as 'The Red Hugenberg' from the power of his propaganda trust, which not only included a number of daily newspapers and newsweeklies, but illustrated magazines, cinema companies, and publishing firms. A number of his newspapers boasted a far larger circulation than even the official Communist Party *Rote Fahne* before the Reichstag Fire put an end to them all. Münzenberg was lucky to be near enough the German frontier to escape the Nazis after the fire by emigrating first to Prague and then to Paris. He probably became the West European head of Agit-Prop at about this time. In any event Münzenberg was left remarkably free to work unhampered by the normal controls and bureaucratic supervision that restricted most Comintern activity elsewhere.

One of his closest collaborators, Arthur Koestler, described the amazing breadth of Münzenberg's accomplishments, all of which became solely devoted to bringing about the fall of Nazism: 'Willi was the Red Eminence of the international anti-Fascist movement. He organized the Reichstag

Comintern's Willi Münzenberg

Counter-Trial – the public hearings in Paris and London in 1933 which first called the attention of the world to the monstrous happenings in the Third Reich. Then came the series of Brown Books, a flood of pamphlets and emigré newspapers which he financed and directed, though his name nowhere appeared. He produced International Committees, Congresses and Movements as a conjurer produces rabbits out of his hat: the Committee for the Relief of the Victims of German Fascism; Committees of Vigilance and Democratic Control; International Youth Congresses, and so on. Each of these front organizations had a panel of highly respectable people, from English duchesses to American columnists and French savants, most of whom had never heard the name of Münzenberg and thought that the Comintern was a bogey invented by Goebbels'.

Willi Münzenberg succeeded beyond his dreams. Not only did his efforts convince the world that a National Socialist gang was responsible for the fire, but he even affected the day-to-day process of the trial. It must be said, however, that neither Münzenberg nor Stalin spared much grief for the fate of Van der Lubbe and Torgler, although the three Bulgarian co-defendants played a rather more important role in their eyes. Van der Lubbe was made a scapegoat by the Comintern just as he had been for the Nazis. Even had Münzenberg so desired, it is unlikely that all of the world's propaganda could have made anyone believe that Van der Lubbe had no part in the adventure at all.

The second man without whom the Comintern would have been virtually defenceless in its fight against the Third Reich was Münzenberg's chief assistant, Otto Katz, who frequently used the pseudonym André Simone. Katz was about forty years old in 1933, a glib journalist with excellent political contacts in the bourgeois world of film makers and society matrons. He became the travelling ambassador of the invisible Willi Münzenberg, a job which incidentally gave Katz ample opportunity to spy on Münzenberg for the central committee of the Comintern. Münzenberg was aware of what Katz was doing, but he contemptuously ignored it. Under Münzenberg's careful guidance, Katz soon commenced a series of regular trips to England and Hollywood collecting money and setting up anti-Fascist committees. These committees played a long and vital role in shaping the 'progressive' fight against Fascism. But Katz's most impressive achievement was his authorship of two remarkable books (closely supervised by Münzenberg): *The Brown Book of the Hitler Terror and the Burning of the Reichstag*, and *The Reichstag Fire Trial: The Second Brown Book of the Hitler Terror*.

The first major effort by the communist *apparat* in Paris was a forgery called the *Oberfohren Memorandum*. It was no coincidence that this document echoed a report first published on 15th March by the French Socialist newspaper *Le Populaire* and which had been refined in other *Le Populaire* articles later in that same week. In fact the source was identical, and it is useful to compare them with the *Oberfohren Memorandum* in order to note the evolution of the Comintern version of the Reichstag Fire.

The *Le Populaire* articles, which were crude by the standards of the Oberfohren forgery, suggested that six or seven Nazis working together with a large German oil company had conspired together in common cause against the Socialist and Communist Parties. The Nazis wanted to discredit the left because of the approaching elections. The oil company barons hoped to drive a wedge which would split off diplomatic and trade relations between Germany and the Soviet Union. Accordingly, Van der Lubbe's passport was specially forged by the Nazis within Germany. Everyone except Van der Lubbe had entered and escaped through the steam tunnels under the Reichstag which led to the palace of the Reichstag President, Göring. The normal staff had been sent off for the day, and Hitlerite troops had occupied the premises.

The *Oberfohren Memorandum* represented a significant advance upon the *Le Populaire* articles. It was 'discovered' fairly soon after the Fire and extracts from it were printed by the *Manchester Guardian* on 27th and 28th April. Eventually the entire document was published by 'The German Information Office', a Comintern front in London, after correcting major flaws that had been uncovered in the original German language invention. The Memorandum was supposed to be the testament of Dr Ernst Oberfohren, the urbane Parliamentary Chairman of the German Nationalist Party, who had committed suicide early in May 1933 over his despair concerning the part played by his party in the coalition of 30th January bringing the Nazis to power. (An alternative view expressed in August in the British press was that Oberfohren's house had been raided by the Storm Troopers who had discovered incriminating papers and virtually forced him to commit suicide.)

Dr Oberfohren was, in fact, an accomplished writer. He had studied at the Universities of Berlin, Bonn and Kiel. Yet the document that he supposedly wrote was obviously the work of 'an uneducated hack'. As his friends reported, Oberfohren might have agreed with a great deal of what was in the memorandum, but he wouldn't have been seen dead writing in that style, using that language, or reflecting such sympathy for the left. He may have bitterly disagreed with Hugenberg, but he was too much the Nationalist to accept the left wing assumptions that underlie the memorandum which bears his name. From other evidence it seems likely that the real author was Albert Norden, former editor of *Rote Fahne*.

According to the forgery, Oberfohren at first despised socialism and

Dr Ernst Oberfohren

communism, but things had changed. He had once rejoiced in the Nazi-Nationalist coalition, but he came to hate Nazism as 'the triumph of barbaric violence' and the harbinger of illegality, disorder and immorality. The Reichstag Fire symbolised in his mind the abominations of National Socialism. The truth must be told in good conscience so that the world might know its mortal enemy.

After the Nazis seized power, says the report, Hitler was tied down by the ponderous institutions that he had inherited; the Stalhelm and Reichswehr were prepared to stand behind the Nationalists under Hindenburg and Papen. The police were 'honeycombed with Social Democratic "sympathisers".' The cabinet powers were weighted unfavorably against the Nazis by the nationalists. Worst of all, the Social Democrats and communists were forming a popular front at long last 'in spite of all the resistance of the Social Democratic leaders'.

Hermann Göring and Dr Goebbels, continued the Memorandum, thought intolerable the paralysis which set into their party after 30th January. Goebbels devised a plan which would permit the Nazis to rid themselves of the nationalist coalition, and at the same time proscribe the Communist Party threat altogether. The first step was to plant incriminating materials in Karl Liebknecht House, which they knew was nearly deserted. A new police President, the Nazi Admiral von Levetzow, was installed in Berlin in order to effect the scheme without the embarrassment of an un-cooperative gendarmerie. With the help of the police the incriminating documents were smuggled into the vacant Communist Party Headquarters. This evidence was then 'found' during the raid of 24th February on the house.

Within two days after the phony raid, the newspapers were filled with horrific accounts describing 'secret corridors, secret trapdoors, passages, catacombs, underground vaults, and similar mysteries'. Nationalist elements within the cabinet were dismayed by the shallow evidence produced by Göring and Goebbels. The nationalists saw through the plot and a terrible argument developed in a cabinet meeting. The rift between the Nazis and nationalists grew.

Goebbels and Göring seethed with rage at the delays. 'They wanted at all costs',. said the Memorandum, 'to force the prohibition of the Communist Party'. The date was finally set for Monday 27th February.

At the appointed hour, Göring's hand-picked agents, 'led by the Silesian SA leader, Reichstag Deputy Heines, entered the Reichstag through the heating-pipe passage leading from the palace of the Reichstag President, Göring. Every SA and SS leader was carefully selected and had a special section assigned to him. As soon as the outposts in the Reichstag signalled that the Communist Deputies Torgler and Koenen had left the building, the SA troops set to work. There was plenty of incendiary material, and in a few minutes it was prepared. All the men withdrew to the President's palace, where they resumed their SA uniforms and whence they could disappear unhampered. The only one to be left behind was their creature, Van der Lubbe, whom they had thoughtfully provided with a communist leaflet on the United Front, a few odd

photographs of himself, and even, it appears, a membership card of some Dutch Communist splinter group.'

That single paragraph, planted in the long, rambling manuscript, provided the focus for which thousands of angry anti-Nazis had been looking. They accepted the truth of the Comintern invention. As late as 2nd August, the *Manchester Guardian* stated: 'While certain details remain mysterious, the complicity of the Hitlerite Government in setting fire to its own Parliament must now be taken as an established fact'. The Oberfohren forgery had the advantage of being exceedingly generalised, so there was little in which it could be contradicted from the information which was available at that time.

Nevertheless, certain aspects of the memorandum did come under attack within the West, even though the story was substantially accepted. It was clear to the more astute observers, such as Torgler's own counsel, Dr Sack, for example, that 'The Cabinet

Left: Karl Ernst at his wedding in 1933, with General Göring and Ernst Röhm
Above: Admiral Magnus von Levetzow: Nationalist, and former Police-President of Berlin, accused by the Comintern of complicity in the Reichstag fire

had no differences whatever of the kind mentioned in the memorandum. It was not the National Socialists who urged the prohibition of the Communist Party, but the German Nationalists themselves'.

Furthermore, contrary to the forgery, there was no chance for the Nazis to have planted the mass of incriminating documents at Karl Liebknecht House. Admiral von Levetzow – a strong nationalist, not a Nazi – and many other policemen would have been required to effect the plan. It is unlikely that the police would have kept such a scheme secret to dupe the nationalist majority in the cabinet. Moreover, the truth was that the raid was first 'planned by a non-Nazi, Superintendent Reinhold Heller, 'a policeman of the old school'. Besides, contrary to the memorandum, Karl Liebknecht House was quite crowded with communist functionaries at the time of the 24th February raid, and there was never any opportunity before that date on which any Nazi plotters might have entered the building undetected by Communist Party officials. Finally, the extensive cache of hidden weapons, presses, and papers discovered and photographed by the police were concealed so carefully that no team could have installed such elaborate devices in the short space of time available to the purported Nazi conspirators.

The violent reaction of the Nazi controlled press to the *Oberfohren Memorandum*, however, exceeded Comintern hopes. When the first excerpts were printed in the *Manchester Guardian*, the *Völkischer Beobachter* screamed, 'This brazen and baseless attack on the Government of a neighbouring state is without equal in the history of any Western nation'. The next day brought even more vituperation: 'The *Manchester Guardian* has openly proclaimed itself a tool of the Communist propaganda machine'. Such hysterical outbursts by the Nazis helped convince most foreign observers that the German Government's infantile tantrums were desperate attempts to conceal the extent of their involvement in the Reichstag Fire.

If the Nazi conspiracy theory was to prevail, the Comintern required some means of amplifying the message contained in the *Le Populaire* articles and Oberfohren Memorandum. Such reinforcement was provided by *The Brown Book of the Hitler Terror*, supposedly written by 'The World Committee for the Victims of German Fascism'. That is to say, it was personally supervised by Otto Katz under the direction of Willi Münzenberg, because the 'World Committee' had no more real existence than the man in the moon.

Albert Einstein was picked by Münzenberg and Katz to be the nominal chairman of the World Committee. Even the *Manchester Guardian* announced Einstein's role in the *Brown Book* as early as 1st June, two months before the book appeared. Actually the eminent scientist refused to have anything to do with the World Committee from the first moment he was asked, but Katz and Münzenberg used Einstein's name anyway. Einstein's protests were ignored by Nazi and Western reporters alike, and Einstein became just another casualty in the great propaganda war.

In the original *Brown Book*, the Comintern sketched Hitler's path to power, its version of Marinus Van der Lubbe's biography, the story of the arson as they wishfully invented it, and the tale of the Nazi terror afterward. The book was perhaps the first published in the English language to damn the Third Reich, and its effect almost surpasses belief. According to Koestler, who assisted Katz, the material for the book came from the intelligence network of the Comintern: 'We had no direct proof, no access to witnesses, only underground communications to Germany. We had, in fact, not the faintest idea of the concrete circumstances. We had to rely on deduction, on bluffing, and on the intuitive knowledge of the methods and minds of our opposite numbers in

the totalitarian conspiracy ... Nevertheless, within a few weeks it was translated into seventeen languages ... and became the Bible of the anti-Fascist crusade.'

The *Brown Book* ingeniously tailored its imagery to fit both the requirements of communist dogma and the predispositions of Western liberalism. It was published in August only a few weeks before the opening of the Reichstag Fire Trial at Leipzig, and it sharply influenced the direction taken by the court. As Koestler suggested, not only was the *Brown Book* so successful that it was translated into seventeen languages within weeks, but it sold millions of copies and 'The *Brown Book* had truly the strongest political effect of any pamphlet since the appearance of Tom Paine's *Common Sense*'.

The book began by describing Hitler's rise to power as the pawn of giant industrial financiers such as Thyssen and Stinnes. After searingly denying Hitler's claim to the slogans and doctrines of 'socialism' and 'revolution', Katz, the real author of the book, carefully drew together the threads connecting Hindenburg and the capitalists with the Nazis. He alleged, as had *Le Populaire* and the *Oberfohren Memorandum*, that Hitler was 'Hugenberg's prisoner'. Then he boldly blamed the Social Democrats for the failure of the united front 'offered' by the communists on 30th January. The left wing in Germany was shattered. Yet Katz claimed that the miracle of resistance was stronger than ever; he said: 'The Hitler dictatorship was opposed by a working class whose fighting strength was as yet unbroken ... the working class answer was the rise of a wide anti-Fascist movement in which all sections were united.'

Katz brought these two behemoths smashing head on: the Nazis' tenuous position worsened day after day; Hitler needed an excuse to correct the

Einstein disowned the World Committee' which claimed him as Chairman

vagaries of his position with the nationalists with whom he was saddled. Katz made the point simple and misleading; he 'logically' established the Nazis' conspiratorial motive which was to stay in power. Hitler needed a provocative act in order to retain power. Because there was no way in which Hitler could escape the 5th March elections which he expected to lose, he had to do something drastic. 'Hugenberg and the German Nationalists held all the economic posts of advantage in the cabinet, the masses of the people were beginning to realise that Hitler was carrying out the policy of the worst firebrands among the capitalists'. The artful Dr Goebbels provided Hitler with 'the plans for the most outrageous of all acts of provocation which a ruling class has ever used against the insurgent working class. Göring was responsible for the exact fulfillment of the plan'. The 'great' coup of the Reichstag Fire was set.

As Katz proceeded, his book launched into wildly ecstatic fantasy. The biographical sketch of Marinus Van der Lubbe was the keystone of the communist theory. According to Katz, Van der Lubbe resigned from the Dutch Communist Party after being threatened with expulsion in April 1931. 'From that date he had no connection whatever with the Young Communist League or Communist Party, but attacked the communists whenever he had the opportunity', Katz wrote. Van der Lubbe was known as a boastful lout, and, it was alleged, 'Enquiries into his life in Leiden have definitely established the fact that he was homosexual'.

These assertions by the Comintern were completely without foundation. Van der Lubbe's real friends in Holland replied to Otto Katz with a book of their own called *The Red Book*. In signed declarations, they refuted the *Brown Book's* lies. The truth was that Van der Lubbe remained at least allied with the communists and retained his friends there. He was not given to idle boasting; on the contrary, he made tremendous efforts to succeed in remarkably ambitious tasks, and his letters to Dutch friends show no sign of boasting.

The *Brown Book* claimed that Van der Lubbe's closest friend, Izak Vink, 'has told our reporter that he has often slept in bed with Van der Lubbe'. But *The Red Book* refuted this libel; Vink proved that he was misquoted and what he really said was, 'I have slept in a bed with Van der Lubbe on a number of occasions *without* noticing the slightest indication of any homosexual tendencies'. *The Red Book* was quite united in this point: Van der Lubbe had never showed himself to be a homosexual. Despite frequent scrapes with the law and his own destitute financial condition, Van der Lubbe had never been suspected of soliciting other men either.

The *Brown Book's* fiction about Van der Lubbe's homosexuality was necessary to provide the vital link between him and the Nazi Party. Supposedly, Van der Lubbe became acquainted with a mysterious Dr Bell on one of the Dutchman's journeys abroad. Dr Bell was supposed to be the foreign affairs adviser to Captain Ernst Röhm, Hitler's SA Chief of Staff. 'Bell was not only adviser in foreign politics to Röhm', claimed the Book, 'he was also his confidant in personal matters . . . it is clear that Röhm was a homosexual. Dr Bell knew many of Röhm's relations with young men, for the reason that he himself procured many of them for Röhm. Bell, who had intimate knowledge of the situation within the National Socialist Party, kept a list of these young men, intending to use it as a weapon against Röhm if any conflict developed with him. Van der Lubbe's name was on this list'.

While it may have been true that Röhm was a notorious homosexual – as common gossip often tells stories about his young boyfriends and his openly soliciting favors of his Storm Troopers – the stamp of authenticity does not extend to their story about Van der Lubbe. Even the London counter-trial, staged under the direction of Otto Katz again, had to damn the allegation attributed to the late Dr Bell as 'not very reliable'.

Nevertheless, the *Brown Book* alleged that from Van der Lubbe's contacts through Dr Bell the Dutchman came into regular communication with the Nazis. The Book says that Van der Lubbe received many letters from Germany and he tried to conceal these from his friends in Leyden. But Van der Lubbe's real friends denied that this was so.

Later, in mid-1932, continued the Book, Van der Lubbe returned to Germany and after renewing his friendly 'relations' with Nazis stayed, for 'he could not bear to stay away'. On 1st and 2nd June it was claimed that he was seen in Sörnewitz in the company of two Nazis, Councilor Sommer and

Herr Schumann where he reportedly admitted being a Nazi and predicted a civil war in Germany. Following the fire, according to Katz's Book, this meeting was reported by Sommer to the authorities after Judge Vogt's offer of a 20,000-mark reward for information. Allegedly, Sommer's tale was reported to Social Democrat functionaries in the Federal state of Saxony. The information was duly forwarded to Frick, Reich Minister of the Interior, and a short time later, Sommer supposedly 'disappeared'. The truth was that the 'Nazi' vagrant in Sörnewitz had long since been identified as someone else.

After his visit in June, Van der Lubbe was supposed to have returned to Holland. He was arrested for smashing windows at the Leiden Welfare Office and jailed. Upon his release, wrote Katz, Van der Lubbe spoke at several meetings in favor of the Fascists. 'We have definite proof of this', the Comintern said. Actually

Ernst Röhm and Karl Ernst (Centre)

Van der Lubbe never spoke for the Fascists at all, and his background, contrary to what was said about his coming from a 'lower middle class' origin, was by no stretch of the imagination comfortable. These were simply *Brown Book* fabrications.

The *Brown Book* further alleged that after his last eye treatment in a Leiden hospital, Van der Lubbe departed for Germany again. When he arrived soon after the Nazis gained power, 'he met the Nazi friends whose acquaintances he had made through Dr Bell'. And Goebbels and Göring now had their willing sacrificial lamb. 'Van der Lubbe's homosexual connections with the National Socialist leaders', wrote Katz, 'and his material dependence on them made him obedient and willing to carry out the incendiary's part. Van der Lubbe's Dutch nationality was a further advantage. It enabled Göring and Goebbels to represent the burning of the Reichstag as an international plot'.

Then Katz detailed the leading figures in the Nazi plot:
'Dr Goebbels: concocted the plot for setting fire to the Reichstag, also the fanatical lies and provocation;
Captain Göring: a drug fiend, directed operations;
Edmund Heines: a murderer, entrusted with the leadership of the incendiary group;
Marinus Van der Lubbe: the tool'.

Meanwhile the Comintern in the *Brown Book* had dropped the phony idea of the forged passport which had been basic to the *Le Populaire* articles. Likewise there was no longer any mention of the oil company. Those two parts of the original version had been too embarrassing: the Dutch passport was verified by Dutch authorities; the oil company would have to be named. The Comintern could not afford to present such a vulnerable profile.

At this point the *Brown Book* repeated the story of the *Oberfohren Memorandum*. Whenever the story lagged or threatened to become transparent, the indefatigable Otto Katz

provided the necessary inventions or illusionary witnesses to plug the gap.

One of the more remarkable 'witnesses' to be pulled out of the hat was the fabulous Berlin magician, and Jew, Eric Jan Hanussen. This man was another real figure who had conveniently died after the fire. Hanussen had felt the way the political winds were blowing about 1930, so he converted to Protestantism and Nazism about that time. He was known to have consorted with a number of high-ranking Nazis. On the eve of the Reichstag Fire, Hanussen held a gala housewarming party in his new flat, which he fondly called 'the Palace of Occultism'. For the occasion a number of well-known Nazi leaders were present, including Count Wolf Heldorff, the Berlin SA Chief. During the party, Hanussen held one of his famous séances. According to Katz, Hanussen told his guests mysteriously, 'I see a great house burning'.

After the fire was put out, Hanussen published an article in the first March number of his weekly newspaper, *Hanussens Bunte Wochenshau*, a piece of literary garbage, in which he discussed the political situation in Germany. According to Katz, 'He wrote in this article that he had known in advance of the Reichstag Fire, but that he was not able to speak openly of it'.

Katz submitted a testimonial by the former editor of the *Berliner 12 Uhr-Blatt*, Dr Franz Höllering, which concluded that 'Hanussen was generally regarded as exceptionally well-informed on National Socialist plans'. The *Brown Book* decided that 'It is clear that some leading Nazi must have given Hanussen information before the Reichstag Fire which enabled Hanussen to "foresee" it. Hanussen must have known a great deal'. But on 7th April 1933 Hanussen was murdered, probably by Nazis.

The story of Hanussen the clairvoyant became popular. A few historians such as the German Harry Wilde, still hold to it. But evidence supporting the idea that someone tipped Hanussen about the fire seems remarkably tenuous. Probably, as Eliot Wheaton has said, the incident was stretched to fit the facts after the event. In any case, Hanussen was a highly vain, sinister and unscrupulous character. While he probably was murdered by Nazis, it is likely that this was for reasons totally unconnected with the Reichstag Fire. He was known to have many connections with criminal society. In his profession it is likely that he had many enemies.

Having thus established the skeleton of a Nazi conspiracy, Otto Katz put flesh on his monster. Using the *Oberfohren Memorandum* again as his point of departure, he took great pains to describe the interior of the Reichstag building and especially its basements. He again drew attention to the steampipe and lighting tunnel which ran to the Reichstag from the boiler plant some distance away. About half-way between each end there was an extension which connected with the Speaker's Residence, or, as the *Brown Book* put it, Göring's house: 'He occupies the house through which, according to his own version, the criminals escaped'.

Not to be outdone by Göring's claim that 'at least ten men' had taken part in laying the fire, the *Brown Book* claimed that Göring's private SA bodyguard consisted of 'at least thirty men'. Katz then trapped Göring with the official Nazi figures that several hundredweight of flammable material would have been required to set the fire adequately. The *Brown Book* erroneously reported that the Berlin Fire Brigade Chief, Walter Gempp, had told officers and men under his command that a truck would have been needed to carry 'a considerable quantity of incendiary material which had not been used', and which Gempp had noticed in the Reichstag after the fire. There is no basis of fact in this story, nor in the falsehood that Gempp was subsequently fired from his posi-

tion because the Nazis were displeased over his behavior and observations at the Reichstag Fire. As a matter of fact Gempp was fired because of his witless malfeasance in accepting bribes from a fire extinguisher manufacturer to the amount of 15,600 marks, and the matter had been hushed up because it was embarrassing to the Prussian civil service.

Next the Comintern pointed out that every door leading into the Reichstag at the street level was locked except Portal Five, where Porter Albert Wendt was stationed. There was no way to enter or escape undetected through any of the entrances above ground. Thus, the *Brown Book* continued. 'The incendiarists would therefore have been obliged to choose some other way, a *secret* way, which would allow them to bring the material into the Reichstag and distribute it at the points required. There is such a secret way into the Reichstag, namely, the underground passage'. Actually the tunnel system was far from secret, but the exact details of its layout could create a certain amount of confusion.

Katz, like Göring, ignored the fact that although the underground tunnel was made of brick, the flooring was mostly of loose corrugated iron plates which could not possibly be traversed without making a tremendous clatter. During the trial the court went to the Reichstag building and witnessed a convincing demonstration which proved that even one man in the tunnel flipping on a lightswitch would make enough noise to alert the staff on duty upstairs. The din caused by thirty conspirators carrying heavy burdens over the rattling iron plates and in a great hurry can easily be imagined under the circumstances. Moreover, far from being a simple straight tube from the Speaker's Residence to the Reichstag, there was a maze of cellars and passages at its terminal points. The policeman whom the Supreme Court sent below during the trial failed to return;

Jan Erik Hanussen: astrologer, magician, and spiritualist here conducting a seance

they had to send a search party after him. According to Douglas Reed, who was with the court and personally visited the steam tunnel himself, 'They found [the policeman] wandering about in the labyrinth below, hopelessly lost'. Katz also failed to mention that a number of locked iron doors barred the way of any trespassers who might have wished to enter the steam tunnels before the fire. Only Scranowitz and his most trusted peole were allowed the keys to those locked doors, and inspection by the police and by expert locksmiths after the fire proved that the locks had not been tampered with. Both sets of keys were accounted for on the night of the fire. Scranowitz had one set in a locked cabinet in his locked office. The other set was found by a police detail consisting of Göring's SA bodyguard Weber and three non-Nazi policemen(picked at random) at 9.36pm.

The police searched the underground system thoroughly – it took them seven or eight minutes – and found nothing suspicious. If Göring had been in any way connected with the cause of the fire, he would not have drawn attention to the 'escape route' by personally ordering a search party within a minute of his hotfooted arrival – that is, before he could even be sure that his minions had escaped.

At this point Otto Katz decided that the guards in Göring's house could hear and see anyone entering the tunnel or leaving it. As a matter of fact this was true, but it was not the Nazi bodyguard who might have seen anything. It would have been Adermann, the non-Nazi night porter at Göring's palace, who later testified that he was in his lodge (which overlooked the tunnel entrance) from 8pm to 10pm without ever leaving his post. Katz, however, suggested that since no communist group would have risked being exposed by the SA gang upstairs, it followed logically that only the Nazis themselves would have used the secret passage! Actually, since the tunnel was effectively sealed by locks and by

at least one nearby non-Nazi witness, a more realistic appraisal would have been that no one used it. If Göring's men had used the tunnel that night, he could easily have replaced Adermann with a storm trooper or a genuine Nazi porter at any time up to the outbreak of the fire. Why should he have hazarded the mission with unnecessary risks? Nevertheless, the *Brown Book* overcame this hurdle by imputing that Adermann was a Nazi and continued, 'No storm troop man would have thought of stopping men who held high positions in his Party and whom he often saw visiting Göring's house. Göring's house was the key position for the attack on the Reichstag. Whoever controlled Göring's house could do what he liked to the Reichstag building. Göring's house was the bridgehead from which the incendiary column advanced to the assault. Göring's house was the depot where the incendiary material was stored. Göring's house was the safe port into which the criminals could flee when they had perpetrated their crime'.

With considerable care Katz argued that only Göring and Goebbels had the authority to plan and execute the scheme. Furthermore they had to find accomplices high in the ranks of the party, since those responsible had to make sure 'the truth' was not revealed. (Notice how this assumption that Göring and Goebbels dared take no risks conflicts with the fact that Adermann and three policemen on the search party were non-Nazis). The next step, Katz explained, was for the incendiarists to assemble outside the tunnel system entrance in Göring's garden and await a special all-clear signal after the last deputy had departed. Then they probably made several trips through the tunnel system to the Reichstag and back carrying their heavy loads of fuel. 'There was no danger of discovery by the Reichstag officials on duty, for these had been sent home by the Nazi House-Inspector [Scranowitz] before the end of their spell of duty'. This again, was a lie. The normal staff was on duty and remained there. The key individuals were non-Nazis. Scranowitz was beyond reproach, and he had been a trusted official of the Reichstag since 1904. Albert Wendt had been the porter at Portal Five for nine years, and Adermann had a similar record.

The *Book*, however, hurried into the last scene. At last the gasoline, tar, and other materials were distributed to the pre-arranged locations according to plan, taking at least twenty minutes. Then everything was set ablaze at once, and the Nazi conspirators retreated down their hole, leaving Van der Lubbe as their willing dupe waiting to be apprehended as an alien communist. What happened to the containers in which the fuels had been stored? The *Brown Book* failed to say. What about Van der Lubbe? 'Van der Lubbe will confess to everything which his employers tell him to confess. He will say against Torgler whatever his employers tell him to say. He will say against Dimitrov everything that is wanted. He will inculpate everyone whom his National Socialist friends wish to destroy. He will exculpate everyone whom his National Socialist friends wish to protect'.

However logical the *Brown Book* may have appeared, there was barely a shred of truth anywhere in the story. Therefore, to render his concoction somewhat more palatable, Katz legitimized the last half of the book by devoting it exclusively to the Hitler terror in every gruesome and familiar aspect. Here he was on much safer ground. The last half of the book is authentic in spirit despite its frequent obeisance to the major communist tenet that the Nazi regime was pro-bourgeoisie. In the final chapter Katz yielded to the temptation of overlooking the pathetic collapse in the left wing workers' movement inside Germany by conjuring up an appearance of the Nazi Party's permanent spectre, the 'still imminent counter-revolution' by the 'tens of thousands of nameless heroes fighting to free Germany and the world from the shameful barbarism of the Brown Shirts'.

Public reactions to *The Brown Book of the Hitler Terror* were mixed. Though many people recognized it as blatant communist propaganda, the most conservative newspapers had to evaluate the startling allegations and sinister conclusions of the book. Much information contained in the *Brown Book* simply appeared nowhere else. The question in every thoughtful reader's mind was whether it could be accepted as true. In an article appearing in *The Political Quarterly* at the end of 1933, Kingsley Martin dealt with this point: 'It is to be noticed that though it was everywhere stated that the case would have been stronger if it had been expressed more judicially and without so large an intermixture of general communist propaganda, there was almost unanimity in the English press regarding the case against Göring and his colleagues as being completely made out'.

Careful dissection of the Comintern version revealed its flaws. But little was known of the true facts at the time. The world was betrayed by half-knowledge and ignorance; it frequently believed something was entirely true if part of it was known to be correct, and it was insufficiently in command of the facts to unravel the skein so artfully wound by the Münzenberg Trust. Otto Katz and Willi Münzenberg's combination of clever rhetoric and brilliant invention glossed over their imperfections. The Comintern themes were incessantly repeated, and as the variations multiplied and grew increasingly sophisticated, the only voices raised in protest came from the Third Reich. But the Nazis had already committed themselves to telling known lies, so they were in no position to complain when their errors were doubled back upon them by the Communist Third International.

London
counter-trial

Caxton Hall on the eve of the Leipzig Trial. Mr D N Pritt, KC, reads the findings of the Commission

Before *The Brown Book of the Hitler Terror* reached the printing presses, Willi Münzenberg and Otto Katz were planning their next step in the Comintern war against German 'Fascism'. In April 1933 the Secretariat of the World Committee for the Victims of German Fascism (Otto Katz) proposed a special inquiry into the Reichstag Fire to identify the real culprits. 'Such a commission', Katz announced, 'composed of impartial and eminent jurists, would be able to throw important light upon the Reichstag Fire and its related events'.

The Comintern Paris *Apparat* approached famous liberals in Europe and America through communist front organizations. A number of well-meaning lawyers were induced to participate in a 'parallel trial', and in some cases where certain men refused to involve themselves, their names were used by the Comintern without consent, just as in the case of Albert Einstein, the 'World Committee's' nominal 'chairman'.

The blue-ribbon committee of celebrated jurists purportedly included Clarence Darrow, Felix Frankfurter, Arthur Garfield Hays, Paul Cravath, David Levinson, Samuel S Liebowitz, and Leo Gallagher from the United States. From England the Comintern involved Denis Nowell Pritt, Neil Lawson, Sir Stafford Cripps, and others. In France they found Henri Torrés, César Champinchi, Vincent de Moro-Giafferi, Marcel Villard, Adolfe Jaeglé, and Gaston Bergery. From the Netherlands they assembled Drs Betsy Bakker-Nort and Van't Hoff-Stokk. In Belgium they appealed to Maîtres Braffort, Graux, Soudan, and Vermeylen. Others included Georg Branting, son of the late Social Democratic Prime Minister of Sweden and a member of the Swedish Parliament; Valdemar Huidt, an eminent Danish advocate; Johannes Huber, Vice President of the Swiss National Parliament, and Pietro Nitti, Prime Minister of Italy before the rise of Mussolini. None of these men were communists. All were staunch defenders of civil liberty. Very few either had time to spare or were tempted sufficiently by the publicity and cause to serve on Münzenberg's kangaroo court. None of those finally selected knew then that the Münzenberg Trust was behind the operation.

Those members of the commission finally selected to judge the case were: Mr Arthur Garfield Hays (USA), Senator Georg Branting (Sweden), Maître Vincent de Moro-Giafferi (France), Mr D N Pritt, K C (Britain), Dr Valdemar Huidt (Denmark), Dr Pierre Vermeylen (Belgium), and Dr Betsy Bakker-Nort (the Netherlands). Herr Johannes Huber (Switzerland) and Signor Pietro Nitti (Italy) agreed to serve, but pressure from their governments prevented their attendance. Clearly Münzenberg was carefully attempting to secure as much of a cross-section of liberal European legal talent as possible. With the exception of Norway, Spain and Portugal, every West European country was represented along with the United States.

On 2nd September the International Commission of Inquiry held a preliminary meeting in Paris. It determined to send three members on a whirlwind tour through Holland to investigate Van der Lubbe's history. The sub-committee spent two days in Holland and was back in Paris by 7th September. Münzenberg, with Katz acting for him like his holy ghost, carefully shepherded and shielded the expedition. Consequently, the results were completely against Van der Lubbe, since every witness had been carefully pre-selected and screened by Otto Katz.

Then on 11th September, only three days before the commission was to hold its first public session in London, an amazing event occurred in Paris. A huge night rally took place in the Salle Wagram. At least 10,000 people were turned away at the doors. Communists in the crowd chanted, 'Death to Hitler, the murderer', and several riots broke out involving police and demonstrators. Henri Torrés and Vincent de Moro-Giafferi's speeches developed the same themes that Katz had presented in the *Brown Book:* Van der Lubbe was a half-blind, half-witted maniac. He had been expelled from the Communist Party for 'Fascist tendencies'. Van der Lubbe was a chronic liar. Van der Lubbe had fallen into the traps of Nazi informers. No sane man could question the fact that Van der Lubbe had accomplices. Torgler and the Bulgarians were innocent for 'No lawyer in the world would consider charges based on such grotesque foundations', as Moro-Giafferi declared. 'There was not a court in the world, no system of justice even the most rigorous, which could hold to the lies invented by the police', he said. Then he asked, 'Who was the criminal mastermind behind the plot?' And he shouted, 'Göring's the one!' The crowd roared its approval, passing by acclamation a resolution which read in part, 'Fifteen thousand citizens assembled at this meeting denounce the parody of justice which is being prepared at Leipzig, noting that for the first time in the annals of the law it is the guilty who arrogate to themselves the right of judging the victims. They salute and place their hopes in the jurists united in London for the ends of high and untainted justice and denounce the quadruple crime which is being prepared in the name of racism and intolerance'.

Such amazing statements coming before the defendants reached their trial were equalled only by Judge Vogt's communiqués to the German press. What chance had truth to emerge then? The object of each participant in the Reichstag Fire Inquiry at London was to perjure the Supreme Court Trial at Leipzig. As D N Pritt candidly admitted in 1965, 'The Counter-trial – more accurately the Reichstag Fire Inquiry – was de-

signed not only to "head off" the trial at Leipzig in the eyes of the world public opinion by ascertaining and publishing the true [sic] facts, but still more to bring the direct pressure of public opinion on the trial court by making public its own fully-reasoned conclusions, based on evidence, before the hearings at Leipzig began'.

The commission began sitting in the chambers of the London Law Society (despite a protest from the British Foreign Secretary, Sir John Simon) on Thursday 14th September, a week before the start of the real trial at Leipzig Supreme Court in Germany. Even the location of the London Inquiry was a stroke of the Münzenberg-Katz genius: the site at 60 Carey Street was nestled beside the Royal Courts of Justice and suitably close to Fleet Street newspaper offices.

The courtroom, which normally had difficulty in holding a mere hundred people, was as carefully staged as the commission itself. Over two hundred people crowded inside. One newspaper reporter said, 'Men and women wedged along the back and the walls, and all through the morning the entrance hall and short passage leading from it to the courtroom were thronged with crowds of people, including witnesses in the case, press photographers, foreign "observers", and almost the entire corps of the continental and United States journalists in London. Admission was by ticket only and those coming in had their cards carefully scrutinized. In the back rows in the courtroom there was a "gallery" of celebrities, including Mr H G Wells, Mr George Lansbury, Miss Jennie Lee, Herr Ernest Toller, Mr Ivor Montagu, and Mr Harold Laski. The number of members of the general public admitted cannot have been more than a dozen or so.'

Münzenberg and Katz wanted to make the scene as attractive as possible. The distracting bustle and noise of the expectant audience was reminiscent of an opening night at the theatre. With everyone's attention partially

George Bernard Shaw. He refused to attend the London Counter-Trial

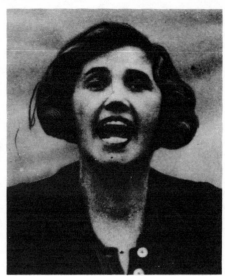

Jennie Lee MP, one of the 'celebrities' at the London Counter-Trial

distracted by one another, the show was ready. As *The Second Brown Book* grandly announced (in language reminiscent of the Russian Revolution): 'Shoulder to shoulder sat the foremost leaders of English thought, of political life, and of the anti-Fascist movement'. But not everyone wanted to be in on the rising curtain of Münzenberg's crusade. George Bernard Shaw, for instance, knew a tragedy of errors when he saw one. He declined a glowing invitation to attend saying, 'Whenever a prisoner is used as a stick with which to beat a Government, his fate is sealed in advance'.

Most public leaders and the press itself were skeptical of the merits of the counter-trial. The commission had to go out of its way in order to convince the world that it was what it was not: an impartial inquiry. There was fear, even in the British Labour Party, that the commission might be led astray by the communists. 'As it was important to convince Western liberal opinion', D N Pritt recalled, 'I and most of my colleagues thought it necessary to hold the Inquiry in the calmest and quietest atmosphere

possible, with a procedure substantially equivalent to that of an English Court'. Consequently, under the chairmanship of Pritt, the courtroom proceedings were lacking in emotion and color. The spectators became increasingly bored, and Moro-Giafferi was disgusted enough to leave the scene after the first day. In the end Pritt's strategy worked, for the world press – even the German press – was impressed by the ponderous solemnity of the occasion.

Sir Stafford Cripps KC, black sheep of the Labour Party, gave the keynote address in somewhat self-righteous tones, noting that the fire occurred 'at a time of great political feeling in Europe and at a time which seemed to suit the political conditions then in Germany'. Due to the resultant terror after the Reichstag Fire, it seemed improbable that the Leipzig Trial could proceed without great difficulty, and he reported that a German newspaper had demanded the death penalty for any witnesses called by the defence. 'In such an atmosphere', said Sir Stafford, 'it is obviously impossible to get witnesses who are antagonistic to the present German regime to enter Germany for the purpose of giving evidence'.

Thus, he continued, the trial inside Germany would 'be a political trial in the fullest sense of the word'. It seemed advisable to constitute a legal commission beyond the German frontier which might establish the 'truth,' seeing that world public opinion had been apprised of the differing interpretations of the fire in German newspapers. Cripps emphasised that material which first gained public attention in the *Brown Book* would be examined by the tribunal. He stated that none of the present committee members had taken part in compiling the *Brown Book*, nor were they responsible for it in any other way. The evidence would come forward, nevertheless, 'so that the public of the world would be able to see whether and, if any, what political motives lay behind the incendiarism of the Reichstag building'.

Evidence revealed by the counter-trial took an unexpected turn quite early. Because Katz and Münzenberg were unable to manipulate the members of the commission as directly as they might have wished, Katz (acting as the World Committee 'Secretariat') chose the witnesses with great care. Naturally, occasional problems arose. On the first day, for an example, a showcase witness who was expected to impress the spectators, a Dr Hertz, who had been a Social Democratic Deputy in the Reichstag since 1920, told the commission, 'On the day of the fire everything was normal in the Reichstag. No precautionary measures were taken'. In other words there were no unusual changes in the staff routine. With that admission made public one of the Comintern's favorite *canards* flew out the window. Even Münzenberg quailed at suggesting that the mysterious incendiarists placed vast quantities of fuel without being heard. Thereafter the Comintern all the more strenuously insisted that the Reichstag staff must have been Nazi pawns. Meanwhile Katz tried harder

to determine what prospective celebrity witnesses might wish to say, and where possible collusion was encouraged behind the scenes for the sake of the anti-Fascist cause.

The second day of the counter-trial. Friday 15th September, Professor Georg Bernhard, former managing editor of the *Vössische Zeitung*, gave the Commission an analysis of the political situation before the fire. He reported that the effect of the Reichstag Fire upon the German populace was 'enormous'. He blamed the government's control over the press and radio for the rapid mesmerizing of the country. When asked by Pritt what political party stood to gain by the fire, Dr Bernhard replied, 'Only the National Socialists could have derived any advantage from the burning. It was obviously out of the question for the communists to have got any benefit from it'. He stated that there had never been a real communist threat to Germany.

Professor Bernhard then submitted a character sketch of Ernst Torgler, describing him as highly reliable and very intelligent; 'It was utterly impossible for a man of that kind to commit a crime such as firing the Reichstag'. The former newspaperman had served two Reichstag committees alongside Torgler while a deputy, and he knew Torgler well. It was not as though the witnesses were sympathetic to the communists. Bernhard indeed described himself as 'violently opposed to communism but sufficiently familiar with the communists to know that they did not go in for individual acts of terror'. Bernhard was forthright, but his testimony served Katz and Münzenberg well.

Bernhard was followed by another celebrity witness, Dr Rudolf Breitscheid, Chairman of the German Social Democratic Party. Breitscheid averred that anyone who knew the political situation in Germany realized that Torgler could not possibly have set the fire. Torgler always expressed very strong personal views against individual acts of terrorism. Although no friend of the communists, Breitscheid noted that the Communist Party had abided by strong appeals by its leaders against individual terrorism since the end of 1931. 'There has never been a communist danger, not even in the month before the fire', Breitscheid declared, 'Whatever one says about the communists, one cannot consider them capable of such a thing. I have known Torgler for many years and have had many talks with him. Although I am his opponent, I must say that he is far too capable to be guilty of such an act of political folly'.

Another staunch anti-communist, Dr Grzesinsky, formerly Chief of the Berlin Police, likewise gave evidence that no communist threat to Berlin existed before the Reichstag Fire. The Berlin police kept well informed of the communists and their movements. It was he who gave the order for Karl Liebknecht House to be searched by police. Every corner of it was known to the police. The great 'catacombs' described in Göring's press releases did not exist. There were only normal basements, though material had been found. Grzesinsky told the inquiry that the Berlin police were prepared to go on to full-scale alert at a moment's notice in case of political trouble. A tactical group of 3,000 policemen could be deployed to any building in Berlin within half an hour.

The counter-trial needed witnesses like Bernhard, Breitschild, and Grzesinsky to maintain its claim to impartiality and authority. Yet Münzenberg realized that he could not depend upon such relatively important men with such substantial characters and reputations to do his bidding. So he steadily filtered through the witness box a variety of seedy individuals whom he could manipulate. One such mysterious witness was Albert Norden, inventor of the *Oberfohren Memorandum*. Norden came disguised as a Storm Trooper with a mask over his face – in D N Pritt's clever phrase 'giving evidence under an alias'. The

Dr Rudolf Breitscheid, a witness at the Counter-Trial

mask supposedly would help the 'informer' to escape the Nazi wrath when he returned home! But more to the point it would allow the witness to escape the recognition of the Western press.

On the third day of the inquiry, Saturday 16th September, Münzenberg launched one of his most important mystery witnesses, a journalist whose name was not revealed. This stranger, formerly of Berlin, proved a sheer disaster for the Comintern. He was supposed to support the hoax about Van der Lubbe, Dr Bell, and Ernst Röhm. The witness bungled the story so badly that the commission disregarded his testimony in utter disgust. Nevertheless the bizarre Dr Bell was quietly tucked away until a more favorable time, and a harmless parliamentary correspondent for the *Vössische Zeitung* was ushered into the courtroom. The reporter, Adolf Philipsborn, had little to contribute, but at least he provided a welcome break from the sordid fables of the previous witness. Then another star witness was brought in, the Communist Deputy Wilhelm Koenen, who was also Secretary-General of the Communist Party in Germany and had been with

Torgler on the evening of the fire. He directed attention once more to the events of the night in question and described the last few hours he had spent with Torgler and Anna Rehme. He also indicated that only by luck had he escaped capture in Germany and expressed fear of being assassinated.

Another series of questionable witnesses scattered throughout the length of the counter-trial were sixteen Dutchmen who gave evidence beginning on the second and third days regarding Van der Lubbe's background. Every one of them was hostile toward Van der Lubbe, and not one varied from the version that Katz had written in the *Brown Book*. Later, at the Leipzig Supreme Court, virtually the same kind of inspired witnesses came forward to clutter the prosecution case, but the witnesses in Germany were Nazi, not communist, and they alleged that Van der Lubbe had attended communist rendezvous in greater Berlin instead of Fascist meetings in Holland.

On Sunday 17th September, the commission went into a ten hour private session and heard witnesses who could not be brought before the public. Katz was not going to give the counter-trial a day of rest.

On Monday 18th September, the commission met again. Ernst Torgler's fourteen-year old son Kurt related how his father had acted on the day before the fire; the elder Torgler told him that the communists would not commit any foolishness during the election campaign, and he had mentioned that some sort of cooperative arrangements should be made with the Social Democrats. Young Torgler then described his father's appearance in Moabit Prison. Then he indicated to the Commission that his mother had experienced great difficulty in obtaining a lawyer with enough courage to defend her husband. One left wing lawyer with excellent connections had reluctantly presented himself to the family for a fee of 5,000 marks. we could not pay this fantastic fee, because my mother receives only 45 marks a month in relief, and we are not allowed to receive any help from the Party. When after much trouble we did manage to collect something on account, the lawyer would not go on with the case.' Ultimately Dr Alfons Sack, a National Socialist lawyer, had been recommended to Torgler, and his services were gratefully accepted. The boy would one day learn that, Nazi or not, Dr Sack was the best lawyer Torgler could have had under any circumstances.

Later during the Monday session the courtroom doors were dramatically locked while Otto Kühne, Secretary of the Reichstag Communist Party group, gave evidence. Kühne declared that it would have been impossible to conceal any incendiary material in the Communist Party rooms upstairs in the Reichstag as the Nazi press was then alleging. Thus any such flammables would have had to be brought past the very noses of the night porter downstairs. Kühne described how Torgler had gone home with him about 1.30am on the morning after the fire. At 6.00am the police had come to arrest Kühne. Torgler, however, left the apartment unquestioned, because the police failed to recognize him. Torgler was just dressing when the police burst into his room, and the embarrassed officers had excused themselves politely and withdrawn, taking Kühne with them. Torgler then finished his breakfast, and later in the morning he gave himself up to the police. Kühne later was able to escape the country. He scoffed at the idea that Torgler had ever met Van der Lubbe in the Reichstag. 'Could anyone imagine Van der Lubbe, who was not a member of the Communist Party in Germany, coming from Holland and saying to Torgler, "Let us burn this place down" and Torgler replying, "We have waited a long time for you; why did you not come earlier?" '

Kühne said only a single charge had

been preferred against Torgler – that he had spoken to Van der Lubbe on the day of the fire and discussed its preparation. Kühne himself was alleged to have participated in the discussion. That was a fiction by the two curious Nazi Party deputies Karwahne and Frey who had taken the Austrian Nazi Kroyer on a tour of the building. Kühne admitted to the London Commission that indeed he had talked to Torgler that afternoon, but the third man was not Van der Lubbe. It was a famous bourgois journalist by the name of Walter Oehme. Far from conversing in an enclosed room such as would presumably have been chosen in a conspiracy, the discussion had taken place in an open ante-chamber to a large hall. A great many people passed through the room on their way to the hall. It would have been folly to set up a conspiratorial meeting without privacy. Karwahne was a crook, and he could be disregarded. Because of certain transactions at the racetrack, Kühne said, Karwahne had been expelled from the German Communist Party. Ever since that time Karwahne had bitterly opposed the Communist Party. Under the circumstances, Kühne concluded, he felt unable to return to Germany and testify at Leipzig on Torgler's behalf. His testimony in London, however, played a major role in substantiating Torgler's own story in Leipzig.

After Kühne had safely departed, D N Pritt read a declaration supposedly executed before a Parisian notary by a woman secretary to a German journalist. This was the strongest evidence that Münzenberg could afford to present in support of the *Oberfohren Memorandum*. The secretary had typed a document from the journalist's dictation based upon information that he had received from Dr Oberfohren, said the affidavit. It declared that the secretary's typed manuscript was identical to the *Oberfohren Memorandum* 'with a few alterations'. Incredibly, the distinguished jurists on the London Commission of Inquiry saw nothing wrong in this deposition. They expressed their pleasure at receiving it, and they were willing to stake their reputations on its truthfulness. It was the cornerstone to their case. If it had been proven that the secretary did not exist and that the journalist was fictitious, then surely that distinguished panel would have begun to realize that perhaps the entire theory contained in the memorandum was an invention. Then, perhaps, they might have asked Why, Whom, and How. They might have re-examined some of the other witnesses. But the blue-ribbon members of the Commission did not question the deposition of the mythical secretary, and so the *Oberfohren Memorandum* became their basic reference, amended as necessary by the *Brown Book*. D N Pritt, in his autobiography, protests that 'we expressly refrained from relying on it, because of doubts as to its authenticity'. However in view of the commission's conclusions it cannot be doubted that Pritt and the others indeed relied extremely heavily upon the *Oberfohren Memorandum*.

In the afternoon of the Monday session Georg Ovijic, a Croatian communist, revealed that on the day before the fire Dimitrov had been in Ovijic's company in Munich. The next day Dimitrov remained in Munich, too. Ovijic said that Dimitrov visited a dentist's office in Munich on both days to have his teeth fixed. On the day of the fire Ovijic introduced Dimitrov to an American girl, Pauline Jarvey, of Jugoslav origin. After Dimitrov was arrested, this girl had offered to give evidence to the Leipzig Court. Dimitrov finally left for Berlin by train at 8pm on the night of the fire. When the fire broke out an hour later, Dimitrov was still on the train.

Several other witnesses including Ernst Toller, the famous German playwright and poet, testified concerning Nazi terrorism and social injustice under the new government. Toller told the court, 'There are thousands of people in concentration camps today who have no idea what they are charged with.'

This was the last public session, at least until the Leipzig trial was in full swing. In the evening the London Commission of Inquiry met privately to consider the results. They concluded late the next night in a state of near exhaustion. Pritt himself worked thirty-six out of thirty-eight hours on the night of the 19th/20th. The main difficulty was in how to word the document. But their decisions were never in doubt. As Fritz Tobias deplored, 'It was in the nature of things that these were the mirror image of the subsequent verdict of the German Supreme Court: where the former blamed the Nazis, the latter blamed the communists'. Both sides failed to show what the German Prosecutor called 'the particular way in which each of the accused carried out the crime'. The deliberate intent of each side was to stage a political trial. There was little room for truth. Political speculation by the judges on both sides

The Reichstag fire Counter-Trial in London

largely had replaced the established canons of evidence and law.

On Wednesday evening, 20th September, the day before the Reichstag Fire Trial began in Leipzig, the London Commission of Inquiry into the burning of the Reichstag announced its preliminary findings. The chairman, Mr Pritt, read the thirty page statement to a large audience in the Caxton Hall, obtained specially for the occasion. Summing up, he said:

'The Commission accordingly concludes on the investigations which it has so far made as follows, (1) That Van der Lubbe is not a member but an opponent of the Communist Party; That no connection whatever can be traced between the Communist Party and the burning of the Reichstag; That the accused Torgler, Dimitrov, Popov and Tanev, ought to be regarded not merely as innocent of the crime charged but also as not having been concerned with or connected in any manner directly or indirectly with the arson of the Reichstag. (2) That the documents, oral evidence, and the other material in its possession tend to establish that Van der Lubbe can-

not have committed the crime alone. (3) That the examination of all the possible means of ingress and egress to or from the Reichstag make it highly probable that the incendiaries made use of the subterranean passage leading from the Reichstag to the house of the President of the Reichstag; That the happening of such a fire at the period in question was of great advantage to the National Socialist Party.

'That for these reasons and the others pointed out in the third part of this report, grave grounds exist for suspecting that the Reichstag was set on fire by or on behalf of leading personalities of the National Socialist Party'.

During the course of the Leipzig trial the counter-trial reconvened several times 'to consider new developments and evidence', but when it finally submitted – and publicized – its final report on the day before the Leipzig trial sentenced the defendants, the conclusions of the counter-trial remained unchanged. There were, however, additional variations to the Comintern themes which had develop-

ed so grandly in the course of the London counter-trial and before. *The Second Brown Book*, published when the trial at Leipzig was over, was the capstone to the efforts of Münzenberg and Katz. A convenient drawing which shows 'the threads leading to Göring' was published in *The Second Brown Book* and demonstrates the comprehensiveness of the Comintern fabrications. The author of the present book has included here a similar diagram refuting each of the Comintern allegations. But facts were insignificant in the political effect of the Comintern version, especially as it became more refined in *The Second Brown Book*. The timing and impact of the most important of these variations made them especially significant. The later postulations and correctives in the Comintern version cannot be divorced from the trial against which they were set. The Comintern offensive against Nazism was above all dynamic, not static, though it often suffered from the paralytic influence of communist dogmatism.

The beauty of the Katz-Münzenberg mythologies lay not in their arrogant finality, nor in their durability, nor even in their evolution from the simple stop-gaps of the articles in *Le Populaire* to the sophisticated *Second Brown Book*. The classic creative genius of the Münzenberg Trust lay in masterful timing, which managed to remain one step ahead of the Nazis all the way. We have suggested in this book that the Nazis triumphed in Germany because they ignored rationality and acted before thinking. But in the end the Comintern succeeded in arousing the world because Münzenberg and Katz did think, they did plan, and they did calculate. The Paris Agit-Prop Office consistently anticipated the gut-reactions of the National Socialists and then used those reactions to further Comintern objectives. In the post-Cold War era, it may be well worth remembering that Münzenberg merely schemed; his enemies lost their reason before they lost their cause.

The Leipzig Supreme Court where the
Reichstag fire case was tried

Supreme Court Trial at Leipzig

Outside Germany people believed that Hitler's gang would never allow the defendants to live to reach an open court of law. But Hitler and Goebbels believed their own propaganda and thought a political show-trial would further their 'revolution'. Thus the Trial of 'Van der Lubbe and Associates' began at the Fourth Criminal Chamber of the Leipzig Supreme Court on 21st September 1933. At the time of the Van der Lubbe Trial the Supreme Court Justices sitting on the bench were not yet *gleichgeschaltet*, nor were they hand-picked for the occasion. The same judges had presided over cases involving communists in past years, but they had also convicted Nazi ruffians of treason before 1933.

There were five justices. The President of the Court was Dr Wilhelm Bünger, who was a prominent figure in Stresemann's tiny liberal *Völkspartei* and until 1930 was Minister President of Saxony. Few could question his allegiance to the Weimar Constitution, but there were some who remembered that Bünger was a politician before he was a judge. His Associate Justices on the case were Justices Cönders, Frölich, Lersch, and Rusch.

The defendants were tried on charges of arson and high treason under the notorious Van der Lubbe Law, passed 29th March – *after* the Reichstag burnt. This Law upset the ancient principle of *nulla poena sine lege* – no penalty except under law – which had formed a basic part of the German Constitution. Unfortunately, Hindenburg's precipitate suspension of German civil rights by his decree of 28th February not only permitted constitutional guarantees to be overthrown, but also set a death penalty for arson of public buildings (or conspiracy for such arson) provided that such arson was caused 'with the intention of provoking an insurrection the outbreak of which was to be in-

The Supreme Court Chamber, scene of the Trial

Dr Bünger, President of the Supreme Court

fluenced or facilitated thereby'. Under such circumstances arson became high treason.

On the morning of the opening session a crowd of thousands gathered in front of the closely guarded court building in Leipzig, but very few persons passed through the police cordons to enter the great hall. The small courtroom off the great hall was brightly illuminated by searchlights for the benefit of the newspaper photographers and cinema newsmen. On Dr Goebbels' instructions a special table was set to record the proceedings on wax discs for nightly radio broadcasts.

Before the proceedings opened at 9.15am, Van der Lubbe and the other four defendants were brought into the courtroom. Van der Lubbe was handcuffed and there were heavy chains round his neck and waist. The others were unbound. None of the five showed signs of physical abuse, although Van der Lubbe's appearance was unfavor-

ably commented upon. Arthur J Cummings of the London *News Chronicle* wrote, 'I do not think I have ever seen any prisoner with such an air of solemn, bovine dejection . . . He had all the appearance of a sour half-wit; and when, some minutes later, the handcuffs and chains were removed, and he suddenly grinned and giggled and rolled his eyes from side to side, it seemed to me more than ever that the proper place for him was not in the dock but a mental home.'

The extraordinary difference between the appearance of Van der Lubbe and the other defendants was likewise subject to much comment. Said the *News Chronicle*, 'Torgler presented a remarkable contrast. He is obviously a man of refinement and education. His clean-cut features reveal intelligence, self-control, and candour. It was as difficult to picture him as it would be to picture Mr Baldwin setting fire to a public building in order to

Ernst Torgler and Marinus Van der Lubbe at the Leipzig Trial

Security guards check witnesses and spectators at the Leipzig Trial

start a revolution.' Meanwhile Popov chattered cheerfully with his interpreter and apparently had great difficulty in following the course of the proceedings. Tanev bore considerable signs of strain, and Dimitrov, who was later to command so much attention, looked worn and anxious.

When the judges entered the courtroom in their square caps and scarlet gowns, everyone rose and gave the Hitler salute. As one English observer wrote, 'In Germany today even the judges are called upon to give this salute. To refuse to do so would be an even greater offense than the refusal of a British judge to rise to the strains of the British National Anthem.'

In his opening address the Court President, Dr Bünger, expressed his indignation at the London inquiry, but he said that the serious challenge to the court's authority would not influence the course of justice. The court refused to be intimidated by outside pressures, he said. Only the present proceedings must determine the court's findings.

Most of the remainder of the day was spent reviewing Van der Lubbe's criminal record and hitch-hikes. Some of the witnesses called and questioned with such formal rectitude struck Van der Lubbe's sense of humor, and he started laughing uncontrollably. The President asked, 'What are you laughing at?' And after a bit of coaxing the defendant replied, 'At the trial'.

Because of growing doubts as to Van der Lubbe's sanity, a series of psychiatric experts were called. Professor Bonnhöffer and Dr Zutt of the Psychiatric Hospital of the University of Berlin, testified that they had examined Van der Lubbe repeatedly and found the witness 'healthy, bodily powerful, talkative, and of ready wit – in fact, he was mentally normal'. They explained that Van der Lubbe's laughter in court was out of contempt for the irrelevant evidence and not from any incoherence of wits. 'He was inclined to burst into youthful laughter, especially when he was asked

questions that seemed to him paradoxical, or others which, in his opinion, complicated simple things quite unnecessarily.' Professor Bonnhöffer also said, in reply to a question from Dr Sack, that Van der Lubbe showed no signs of being unusually susceptible to outside political control. The long imprisonment, however, had left him in a state of acute exhaustion. Besides Van der Lubbe had gone on a hunger strike in hopes of so debilitating himself that the trial could not continue. Between February and July he had lost twenty-five pounds, regaining only a little of it during October and November. As for the persistent rumor that Van der Lubbe had been drugged with scopolamine or hypnotized, they said, 'Even if someone could be kept under hypnosis for weeks and months on end, Van der Lubbe's attitude, behavior, and intransigence are by no means those of a hypnotized or drugged subject'. Dr Zutt concluded that Van der Lubbe's condition was perfectly to be expected; it was only 'the reaction of an unusual man to an unusual situation'. On 27th September, a Swedish criminologist, Dr Södermann from the University of Stockholm, told the Court that he had examined Van der Lubbe in prison and found him exceedingly thin but without any evidence of ill-treatment, hypodermic injections, or slow poisoning. Dr Södermann said, 'I gained the impression that we could have conversed for hours, and that I would invariably receive intelligent and logical answers'. Other psychiatrists and a Dutch journalist testified to the same effect.

The most crucial alterations in the prosecution case came as a result of the testimony of the 'fire experts'. Several of these gentlemen persuaded the court to reject Van der Lubbe's assertion that he had set fire to the building alone. Urged on by the Nazi press and Göring's fantastic accusations immediately after the fire, the court yielded to the tempting testimony of the experts as all other evidence of any conspiracy lagged. Professor Emil Josse, a lecturer in thermodynamics at Berlin Technical College, Dr Wagner, a Berlin Fire Chief, and Dr Wilhelm Schatz, an unknown chemist with a dubious professional reputation, agreed in court that several accomplices were probably necessary. Wagner and Schatz insisted that Van der Lubbe had no time to make adequate preparations in the brief period he remained inside the building. But Professor Josse, in answer to Dimitrov's question, said Van der Lubbe might have been telling the truth up to a point. 'When I saw the speed with which Van der Lubbe broke through the windows during the on-site inspection', said Josse, 'and when I was told that he was in a lather of sweat when arrested, I concluded that he might have done it with adequate preparation'. But when Josse clarified what he meant by sufficient preparation, he asserted that at least forty pounds of liquid fuel must have been spread about by at least two people a half hour in advance. He hypothesized that the fuel had been cached far in advance in the stenographers' room below the dais. The fuel he suggested used was a 'liquid hydrocarbon' such as gasoline or paraffin. Firelighters, he said, were not sufficient, but the liquid fuel when soaked into the wooden seats and panelling would have done the trick; the vapors mixing with the air would raise the temperatures high enough to kindle everything in the room. Then the glass dome would burst with the heat and pressures, causing the explosion at 9.27pm.

The testimony of Dr Schatz was equally technically striking. The building, he said, was prepared with a self-igniting liquid (which he refused to name). His chemical analyses of soot at the scene confirmed his hypothesis, he claimed, but he allowed no one to see his conclusions. The self-igniting fuel was supposedly timed to go off after it was set. In addition fuel oil or paraffin must have been poured all over, but not more than a gallon was used. The arsonists were professionals in starting fires. Their clothing would have reeked from the stench of the fuels used. Van der Lubbe, to Schatz, was a mere tool of the others. He had taken no part in the operation itself, and besides, he was insane. Schatz said, 'In his walks around he probably did not intend any fire at all, but dropped his flammatory material by accident'.

Fire Chief Wagner then testified to having experimented with chairs, tables, and other furniture similar to that which had been destroyed in the Plenary Chamber. Even when prepared with flammable celluloid film and gasoline, they hardly burned. Only vast quantities of fuel, he concluded, would have succeeded. Van der Lubbe must have been helped by at least three other people.

These three expert witnesses bent the facts to suit their fanciful conclusions. Closed buildings, like theatres and dance-halls, present notoriously grave fire hazards simply because their size permits air to mix with the vaporous unburned byproducts (smoke) in case of a fire inside. This mixture becomes critically unstable as the temperature and pressure rise inside the enclosed chamber. Even at normal temperatures, with relatively minor changes between atmospheric layers, winds can reach speeds in excess of a thousand feet per minute (11 – 12mph). However, in a large high-vaulted room like the Reichstag there are usually no wind currents, but there are gradations of temperature from floor to ceiling. So when smoke became superheated in the fire, the destructive potential was enormous as the draughts grew and the smoke thickened. Then all that was needed was a single spark, and everything within reach of the fire provided it fuel – even things which were normally resistant to flames. In the Reichstag there was no place for the gases to escape at first. But when the roof cracked it was like opening a hot oven door in an oven-fire. There was a momentous concussion as the unburnt smoky gases erupted (the same explosion as at 9.27pm).

As Professor Josse indicated, the high kindling temperatures were essential. But the three fire experts were unable to explain the natural fuel already in the Plenary Hall. Dr Schatz tried to rise to the occasion with a dramatic demonstration to 'prove' that Van der Lubbe could not have set the fire using only the little which he had. Schatz got some samples of fireproof curtains matching those which had burned, then he tried to light them. Presto! They refused to burn. Everyone was impressed – obviously, they thought, Van der Lubbe could not have set the fire. Or could he? The fireproof curtains had been taken from storage in heavy chests where they had lain undisturbed for years in virtually airtight, light-proof location. The condition of these samples explains the reason why Schatz' curtains did not burn on cue.

Berlin Fire Brigade Director Walter Gempp testifies at the trial

A government chemist by the name of Dr Lepsius had told the court that the plush velvet curtains which Van der Lubbe ignited had been installed decades previously and had never been dusted. Fireproofing wears off from constant exposure, variable humidity and temperature, simple use, and dust Dr Lepsius correctly concluded that the Plenary Sessions Chamber had ignited after the flames from the musty curtains first preheated and then leapt the distance to the bone-dry wooden panelling. Unfortunately, the court was so awed by Dr Schatz' demonstration that it failed to give weight to Dr Lepsius. Neither was Chief Fire Director Walter Gempp's statement weighed: 'The dessicated old panelling offered the fire excellent food, and that is why the fire spread so quickly'.

Moreover, four fire experts reported that their tests showed absolutely no evidence of any residue from liquid hydrocarbons. Firemen, policemen, Reichstag officials, and other witnesses further testified that they smelled no volatile liquids of any kind. (Yet Dr Schatz had told the

Court that the odor of his mysterious fluid would hang in the air for hours!)

It seemed to be more of a mystery, to those in the court who did not believe a lone arsonist had caused the Reichstag Fire, that evidence could be given by other witnesses discrediting the elaborate conclusions of Schatz, Josse and Wagner. For example, Dr Ritter, a government technical officer, said that liquid hydrocarbons never produce the kind of flames and separate little bundles of flames described by witnesses, and that if such volatile substances had been exposed to the air in separate locations for the periods hypothesized by Schatz (over an hour), then the arsonist who tried to light the fire would have little chance of escaping serious injury and the entire place would have gone up like a bomb.

The stenographers' well where the fuels were supposedly stored had been thoroughly cleaned by a charwoman on the afternoon of the fire. Scranowitz himself had inspected it. The elevator attendant had gone there to wind the clock in the afternoon. None of these witnesses had seen any suspicious packages or materials. Yet the court preferred to remember Scranowitz's fantastic story of forty separate little fires, each eighteen inches in size and five feet apart, blazing like little campfires on the deputies' desktops. The court never stopped to think that the House Inspector might possibly have seen the reflections of the central fire off the highly polished wooden desktops, that the angle from which Scranowitz saw those 'little fires' made such an interpretation probable, and that the length of time Scranowitz stood gazing inside before slamming the door closed in the shimmering heat was at most a few seconds. The court did not even try to account for the differences between Scranowitz's observations and those of Losigkeit and Graening a minute earlier. The court took little cognizance of the fact that Van der Lubbe managed to re-run the entire route which he had described for the police, that he did this within the times he had described, and that he could account for every place where examination proved there was a seat of fire. If only anyone would listen to him! Perhaps most unfortunate of all, the court disregarded the evidence of the upholsterer Otto Borchardt, who declared that a tiny fragment of cloth which had stuck to Van der Lubbe's coat matched a drapery behind the stenographers' table.

So the court took the conclusion of the fire experts Josse, Schatz and Wagner that Van der Lubbe must have had accomplices and that it only remained to identify who they were.

From there Dimitrov might well storm to his feet and, pointing an accusing finger at Van der Lubbe, cry: 'This man is the Faust of the Reichstag Fire! But who are his accomplices? We, his innocent co-defendants, demand to know that! The only man in the court who knows the truth, this miserable Faust, will not speak! He remains mute!' As that cry echoed round the world, the Leipzig Supreme Court could neither prove that the fire was a communist plot nor convince the critics of the court that the Nazis were innocent of the crime.

The case against Torgler rested mainly upon circumstantial evidence which was painstakingly taken apart by Torgler and his counsel, Dr Sack. As *The Second Brown Book* remarked, 'Against one of Torgler's calibre and personality the accusations formulated in the official press bulletins were pitifully inadequate for a public trial.' The case finally centred around three issues: firstly, that Torgler had taken part in the arson; secondly, that he was connected in some way with Van der Lubbe and the three Bulgarians; and thirdly, that under orders from the German Communist Party he had tried to inspire others to burn the Reichstag as a revolutionary 'beacon'.

Dr Werner, the prosecutor, suggested that Torgler had used the Communist Party rooms to store the incendiary materials. But the night watchman, Rudolf Scholz, testified that there was no such flammable material about at the time he made his last rounds, a few minutes before Torgler, Koenen and Anna Rehme left for Aschinger's Restaurant. Willi Otto, the postman, agreed with Scholz. Once Torgler arrived at Aschinger's, his presence was accounted for by two waiters, the manager, a cook, and a patron of the restaurant, and at least one of those witnesses was a National Socialist!

On the serious charge that Torgler connived with the others, three witnesses supposedly saw Van der Lubbe and Popov with Torgler on the afternoon of the fire in the Communist Party's chambers. Cross-examination of Karwahne, Frey and Kroyer proved that their testimony was worthless, and other witnesses convinced the court that Torgler had not received Popov or Van der Lubbe in the Reichstag.

It was also proven beyond doubt that the two individuals with Torgler that afternoon were the former Socialist Party Secretary Jakubowitz, who looked surprisingly like Van der Lubbe, and Dr Neubauer, a former communist deputy with a striking resemblance to Popov. Dr Neubauer himself was brought from a concentration camp to tell the bench that he was with Torgler that afternoon, had seen Karwahne and the others. Walter Oehme, a Social Democrat, and two women employees in the Reichstag, Frau Baumgart and Fraulein Derx, as well as a large number of persons likewise testified being with Torgler that afternoon, and they said that neither the Bulgarians nor Van der Lubbe had appeared.

Finally, even the Public Prosecutor could no longer admit to supporting the indictment's claim that Van der Lubbe was seen with Torgler in the Reichstag.

The other accusation that Torgler had long hoped to burn the Reichstag was based largely upon the allegations of Gustav Lebermann, a convicted thief and con-artist, who said that Torgler had been trying for a long time to set him up as a scapegoat in an attempt to burn the Reichstag. Bebermann said that Torgler had promised him a bribe of 14,000 marks in 1932 for the 'big job', but when Lebermann had refused, Torgler had slugged him in the stomach. Ever since then, Lebermann claimed, he had suffered from chronic abdominal haemorrhages. However, the court once more rejected the prosecution's witness, saying that it could be shown Lebermann had long suffered from ulcers and that 'no credence whatsoever can be given to the evidence of the witness Lebermann . . . whom the Hamburg County Court has previously described as being of weak character and a morally inferior person.'

An ex-communist miner and sex criminal, Otto Kunzack, alleged next that he and Torgler had tested some dynamite in a forest near Berlin, but Torgler absolutely rejected this and said that he had never heard of Kunzack. Then the court discovered that Judge Vogt had granted Kunzack a remission of a prison sentence in return for his testimony. The prosecutor forlornly insisted their witness was reliable, but the bench declared that Kunzack was completely untrustworthy. Kunzack also declared that Van der Lubbe, the well-known communist leader Heinz Neumann, and several other communists had discussed terrorist tactics at Dusseldorf in 1925, but Van der Lubbe (who would then have been fifteen years old) had never been to Düsseldorf until 1933, and Kunzack failed to identify a photograph of Heinz Neumann handed to him by Justice Cönders.

On the claim that Torgler had hoped to build a revolutionary front with the Social Democrats to smash the Hitler Government, the news-

Frau Torgler testifies concerning her husband's activities before the fire

Reichstag Director *Geheimrat* Galle gives his evidence to the Leipzig Court

paper articles written immediately prior to the fire, and used by the prosecution, indicated no revolutionary incitements beyond the usual pro forma communist slogans.

Clearly, the circumstantial indictment against Torgler was crushed, and the court had shown itself remarkably independent in his case.

The two Bulgarians, Popov and Tanev, could not speak German. Popov had acquired a rudimentary reading knowledge of German, but Tanev possessed no understanding of the language at all. Thus they could only conduct their defence through an interpreter, and they had to rely upon their lawyer, Dr Teichert. They had no idea of how accurate a translation they were getting or what was happening at any given moment. Popov and Tanev were further disadvantaged by the stubborn refusal of their fellow Bulgarian defendant, Dimitrov, to conduct his defence in harmony with their wishes and the best judgment of their lawyer. As Dr Teichert explained to the court, with an ironic bow to Dimitrov (who was left speechless): 'I conduct the defence as I think right and not as Dimitrov thinks right. As official defender I also have duties to Popov and Tanev who, as Dimitrov knows, do not agree with his dictator's way of conducting the defence.'

The witnesses against Popov included the infamous trio, Karwahne, Frey, and Kroyer, but when they were discredited by Dr Sack and Torgler, Popov was cleared. More serious, however, were the accusations of the engineer Paul Boghun, who had been prompted by the Examining Magistrate, Paul Vogt, to describe Popov as the man Boghun had seen running from Portal Two shortly after nine o'clock on the night of the fire. When the prosecutor and the bench became embarrassed by Boghun's elaborate decorations upon what he had seen, Dimitrov rubbed salt in their wounds by jeering, 'The witness is an engineer, and engineers generally have an excellent memory. However this witness Boghun has remembered much better and more precisely three months after the Reichstag Fire than on the same day of the fire! But for the witness Boghun that's all quite in character! He's a novelist, not an engineer!'

A long-time communist, Otto Grothe, an important Agit-Prop leader in Berlin, declared that a man named Kempner had admitted carrying fuel for the fire into the Reichstag and delivering it to Popov. Grothe also affirmed that Torgler, Thälmann, Popov, Koenen, and other communists held a dress rehearsal for the fire in the nearby Tiergarten on 27th February, the day of the fire. All of this hearsay evidence was admissible in the German court, but cross-examination later revealed gaping holes in Grothe's story, and he was completely discredited. The President of the Court angrily accused the witness of speaking 'garbage' and Grothe narrowly missed being arrested for perjury.

Another witness, a Nazi block warden by the name of Jung, alleged he had been keeping the apartments of a communist underground worker known as Oscar Kämpfer under surveillance with field glasses. Nazi block wardens were normally used in this way to spy on their neighbors. Jung told the court that he and his wife saw Popov visit Kämpfer's apartment and that later certain parcels were delivered there which looked like they contained machine-guns. When this 'evidence' was questioned in court, the Nazis scoured their concentration camps and came up with Kämpfer himself, who by this time could be 'persuaded' to say Jung's testimony was true and that furthermore Kämpfer and Tanev were old comrades. Kämpfer said Popov had been brought to him for shelter by another Communist Party member, and that Popov had been hidden with him at various times in May, June, July and November. Kämpfer swore that Tanev had visited Popov in May and that in July Popov performed mysterious chemical experiments with bottles which made the room stink of gasoline. Luckily for Popov, other witnesses were able to prove that Popov was safely in the Soviet Union during the times mentioned, and Tanev protected his own alibi with witnesses who proved that he was in Sofia and that his first trip to Germany was begun on 24th February. Kämpfer was then exposed as a burglar and a liar who would undertake any invention to escape his fate in the concentration camps. Dimitrov was particularly incensed that Kämpfer was never before expelled from the Communist Party.

The proprietor of a Lindenstrasse cafe, Michalski, and his waiter, Hyta, likewise allegedly saw Popov and Tanev together in Berlin during 1931 and the summer of 1932, but once again witnesses brought forward by the two defendants proved that Michalski and Hyta were mistaken, at the very least, since Popov was either in Moscow or in a Crimean sanatorium throughout the summer of 1932, and his passport revealed that he had first come to Berlin on 3rd November 1932.

A fat seventy-two year old lady by the name of Frau Hartung then charged Popov with being the lover of a friend of hers, Frau Ryschkowski, in 1928, but when Frau Ryschkowski was examined, she furiously denied the story and accused old Frau Hartung of having an affair with her lodger. As the *Second Brown Book* chortled, 'It appeared that these two ladies were on terms none too friendly'. Frau Hartung also made a feeble attempt to attack Dimitrov, but it failed miserably.

Then there was a Jewish merchant, Leo Weinberger, serving a two year sentence for bribery, who related conversations he had in prison with Popov after Popov had been arrested in connection with the Reichstag Fire. Popov supposedly told Weinberger that 'he had often been in Germany before' and 'he was absolutely innocent of the Reichstag Fire, though he might be found guilty of offences against the currency laws, and possibly of high treason'. Weinberger told another prisoner, Wolff, what Popov said. 'Thereupon', said Weinberger, 'Wolff unfortunately took advantage of these remarks, and I was called as a witness'. Dr Bünger angrily protested that Wolff's tattling 'was his duty as a German', but it later came out that Wolff was a professional eavesdropper, and Weinberger, too, was caught in a number of uncomfortable lies. For instance Weinberger reported that Popov had asked him to instruct Weinberger's wife to telephone Popov's landlady so that she might destroy secret papers which the Bulgarians had left in his rooms. But it turned out that Popov's landlady had no telephone. Needless to say, Weinberger was put back into prison and presumably into oblivion.

The most important witness against Tanev was a retired army major, Hans Weberstedt, who was employed by the Nazis as their parliamentary press agent and was a friend of that other Nazi journalist, Dröscher. Weberstedt blustered his way into the courtroom to accuse Van der Lubbe and Tanev of being in the antechamber of the Reichstag Communist Party on the afternoon of the fire. When Tanev accused Weberstedt of lying, the Nazi screamed, 'A retired German officer does not lie, nor does he make mistakes'. Tanev then ticked off the fallacies in the retired officer's testimony, and soon Weberstedt started embroidering a byzantine fantasy. Finally the Prosecutor called a halt, and Dr Bünger, the Court President eventually declared that Weberstedt's 'belief that Tanev was the right man was not spontaneous, but the result of long reflection . . .

Weberstedt probably confused Tanev with the witness Bernstein, especially as he claimed to have seen Tanev in the Reichstag frequently when, in fact, Tanev had only entered Germany on 24th February'.

Another witness against Tanev was Sönke, Tanev's landlord a week before the fire. Sönke, a former communist, asserted that Tanev was an old comrade whom he had known in Rumania. He said they happened to cross paths at the Friedrichstrasse in Berlin and Tanev then came to stay in Sönke's home. This was a relatively unimportant falsehood, but Tanev called out in Russian from the prisoner's box, 'Why are you lying? Tell the truth! Nothing will happen to you'. When this was translated for the court, Dr Bünger took a keen interest and Sönke finally broke down and admitted that Tanev was introduced to him quite recently by a friend of Popov's, and that Sönke had never seen Tanev before then. He sobbed, 'I did not want to become involved in the affair'. For his stupid lie Sonke was sentenced to three years of hard labor, a far harsher penalty than that exacted by the court against Nazis whom they discovered in perjury.

The last star witness against Tanev and Popov was the Bayernhof Restaurant waiter, Johannes Helmer, whose silly testimony was discussed in an earlier chapter in connection with the unseemly Judge Vogt. As Dr Teichert, the Bulgarians' counsel, justly remarked, 'The fact that the Examining Magistrate undertook the prosecution of the three Bulgarians on the basis of this statement has gravely injured the reputation of the German people in the eyes of the world outside.' And when Justice Bünger found out from Helmer that 'thousands of people' sometimes came to the Bayernhof to dine, the court gave up in disgust.

The prosecution of Dimitrov began on the same note as the other Bulgarians. But when Dimitrov rose in the dock to testify, everything changed. As Otto Katz wrote admiringly, 'From that moment his personality stood out head and shoulders above his judges and his prosecutors. He became the shining light of the trial to the world, and to millions the symbol of the battle which was being fought at Leipzig, a hero of the struggle against Fascism'.

The President of the Court, of course, was forewarned. He had read the huge transcript of the preliminary hearing, so he knew that Dimitrov might easily prove the test of his judicial career. And so it became. Dimitrov attacked the prosecution case with relentless fury. But not content with proving himself innocent, he ripped into the court itself, the police, the Nazi Party, the German press, the government ministers, and virtually every other German social institution. Whenever Dimitrov came to speak an expectant silence fell over the courtroom. He was fearfully hated yet begrudgingly

While Dimitrov carries on the battle, Van der Lubbe slumps in dejection

admired by the very men whom he attacked most viciously, and many newsmen present could smell the perspiration that wreathed the brows of the Justices and Attorneys when Dimitrov called them out. The case for the Third International was never more challenging, the repudiation of the National Socialists never more contemptuously expressed. He used the courtroom for a pulpit, and his sermons left his foes incoherent in rage. On the very first day of his examination, he brought the President of the court to silence with an imperious wave of his hand: 'I am a proletarian revolutionary. I am a socialist revolutionary by conviction. I am not of that type of socialist among whom is numbered the German ex-Crown Prince. I am a member of the Central Committee of the Bulgarian Communist Party and of the Executive Committee of the Communist International. I may therefore call myself one of the leaders of the Communist Movement and in such capacity I undertake here and now responsibility for all decisions, all publications, and all activities of

the Bulgarian Communist Party and the Communist International. This, moreover, is the reason why I am not to be regarded as a mere terrorist adventurer. I am an enthusiastic supporter of the proletarian revolution, because I realize that it presents the only way out of the crisis of capitalism.'

When the President of the Court told Dimitrov that a death sentence had been passed upon him by the Bulgarian authorities, Dimitrov shrugged it off with withering scorn: 'I have heard that was the case. I have not made further enquiries because the matter was one which did not interest me'.

Dimitrov's bold impertinence, his utter disrespect for the court were not in the least disguised. His sneers were too insistent, his taunts were too dissecting to be ignored. But with what weapons of evidence was the prosecution armed?

Helmer, the Nazi Bayernhof waiter; Dröscher, the Nazi journalist; and Frau Hartung, the prevaricating dowager were buried beneath his disgust. Six other waiters at the Bayernhof who were not Nazis exposed Helmer's lies. The Bulgarian Government repudiated Dröscher's story that Dimitrov had engineered the Sofia Cathedral outrage. Employees of the communist relief agency 'Red Aid', though shaking with fear for their lives, denied Frau Hartung's hesitant assertions that Dimitrov was a clearing agent for assistance payments. The court was forced to reject the testimony of all three of these prime witnesses for the prosecution.

Who else remained to be slaughtered? Anna Meyer and a chauffeur named Thael claimed to have seen Dimitrov near the Reichstag before the fire broke out, but the Prosecution dropped them scarcely after the ink was dry on the indictment. A Reichstag day-time porter, Wilhelm Hornemann, who had reduced the public to hysterical laughter by

asserting that one of the Reichstag Deputies, Koenen, had tried to 'sneak' into the Reichstag on the day of the Fire, later made an even more ridiculous assertion in claiming to have seen Dimitrov puttering round the Reichstag muttering – in broken German – 'The Reichstag is going up in the air in fifteen to twenty minutes!' At this Dimitrov grinned from ear to ear; the whole world knew how well Dimitrov spoke German. And, of course, he had an air-tight alibi with his presence in Munich established on the day of the fire, and several witnesses who vividly remembered him on the pullman car back to Berlin that night (the car attendant, Otto Wudtke, and a passenger with whom Dimitrov flirted, Mrs Irmgard Rössler).

Because Georgi Dimitrov had an established alibi, he could well afford to turn his brilliant mind to political counter-demonstrations. On the very first day, Dr Bünger rebuked Dimitrov with the words, 'For what reason do you imagine you have been really brought here?' To which Dimitrov retorted, 'To defend Communism and to defend myself!' In that cause Dimitrov was tremendously successful, and every echo of his remarks was repeated by the Münzenberg Trust, the entire Western press corps, and even the German news media.

Dimitrov was expelled from court five times, and considering the flammatory nature of his comments, the court showed remarkable restraint. Not only was the defendant discrediting the court, he was trying his best to prove that the National Socialists were to blame, and here he picked up the themes of the *Brown Book,* the *Oberfohren Memorandum,* and the other Münzenberg concoctions. He was unable to acquire these things directly, but he read about them in the Nazi newspapers.

On the occasion of his first expulsion, 6th October, Dimitrov shouted, 'This affair is a police frame-up!' Later he committed the unforgivable sin of impugning the honor of German officials. He scolded the police for being 'ignorant' because they were so slow at discovering the secret combinations of some inverted telephone numbers in a book found hidden in his room. He called Police Lieutenant Heisig a liar, and he suggested that the police had forged some pencil crosses in a traveller's guide to Berlin which was found: 'It's my book, but I can't guarantee what the police have done with it.' Finally, when he again insisted that 'The police have shown great incompetence and incomprehension', it was the last straw, and the president, after a short consultation with the other justices, said simply, 'Dimitrov will be removed at once and taken back to prison'.

As a matter of fact the forged crosses were of particular importance, since they were opposite the Imperial Palace, the Reichstag, and the Dutch Embassy. As Tobias pointed out, 'Dimitrov had been somewhat impertinent, but when all was said and done, his head was hanging by these idiotic and, to say the least, suspicious pencil crosses on the map'. Moreover, the excited police had exceeded the law in their search of his room. They failed to meet the exacting requirements of the Criminal Code in not producing independent witnesses to the search, not conducting the search within sight of the suspect or his representative, not giving the suspect an inventory of what they seized, and in neither sealing all the evidence inside envelopes nor requesting the suspect or his representative to do so. As a result the court unhappily felt obliged to rule all evidence discovered in Dimitrov's room inadmissible by the standards of law.

Dimitrov insisted upon acting in his own defence without counsel and directly asked questions in court. The Legal Code prohibited this. Dimitrov could have availed himself of Dr Teichert, who was ably defending

Popov and Tanev. But Dimitrov refused to bow to German legal propriety, and he was excluded again for this. Then he wrote a defiant letter to the Court President, saying, 'These exclusions . . . serve to show the world that my accusers are not at all sure of their own case. The expulsions thus only serve to add further substance to existing communist allegations about this trial'.

Dimitrov's argument was telling, and for the time being it won him Dr Bünger's tacit permission to defend himself and use court files.

By the end of October Dimitrov was again emphatically insisting that he had done no more in Germany than the Nazis' agents abroad. 'I worked in Germany as a Bulgarian Communist,' he said, 'as many hundreds of Nazis work elsewhere, with false passports and addresses, for the Austrian Nazis'. Another tactic that seemed guaranteed to annoy the court every time was when Dimitrov mockingly told Nazi witnesses not to be ashamed of themselves. Through these means he managed to goad the justices into verbal conflicts which always left the court in a worse position. So long as Dimitrov was in court, the advantages were all his.

On 1st November, however, a less humorous sally took place which caused Dimitrov to be excluded for the third time. *Völkischer Beobachter* had been livid the previous morning because the court did not take action against Dimitrov for saying 'The chain of witnesses for the Prosecution against us communist accused, which began with Nazi deputies, and continued with Nazi journalists, is now completed by thieves'. The Nazi press had warned gravely, 'We National Socialists hope that even Dr Bünger's court will in future find the means to repress such filthy outbursts from a communist criminal against National Socialist witnesses'. Notice the word 'even'. Dr Bünger took the Nazi warnings seriously, and he told Dimitrov that although

he had not heard the remark in question, he would have done something drastic if he had, and in future Dimitrov must circumscribe his remarks. Dimitrov saucily replied, 'Now the *Völkischer Beobachter* ought to be satisfied!' Dr Bünger was at once convulsed with rage at the implication that the court was a Nazi slave, and as the courtroom erupted in pandemonium, Dimitrov was again hurried out the door, protesting. That afternoon a Nazi newspaper ominously said, 'There is every reason to punish the impertinence of Dimitrov by measures which will leave him no desire to continue his well-thought-out tactics'.

On 3rd November Dimitrov reappeared, still unchastened. But the court was now allergic to Dimitrov, and he was once again snatched from the room at the discomfited Dr Werner's request almost immediately.

The next day Dimitrov was back, despite the fact that Dr Bünger had excluded him for two days. Apparently the court had been given an order from its political superiors, because the grand moment of the trial had

Göring was a witness in the trial, but his bluster was lacerated by Dimitrov

arrived, and no one wanted Dimitrov to be absent. Hermann Göring, Prime Minister of Prussia, Minister of the Interior for Prussia, Air Minister of the Reich, President of the Reichstag, and now a General, came to court to defy Dimitrov and the *Brown Book*. Here, surely, was a real champion who could destroy the bantam Dimitrov! Here was a moment when history would stand still.

In the left corner stood Dimitrov, who would eventually rise to command the entire world-wide operations of the Communist International and then become Premier of Communist Bulgaria. In the right corner stalked Göring, who thirteen years later showed his mettle in making Mr Robert H Jackson, a United States Supreme Court Justice and the American Chief Prosecutor at Nuremberg, beg the International Tribunal for mercy to spare him from Göring's brilliant defence.

Knife-edged nervousness cut through the tense crowd. The courtroom and neighborhood were teeming with carbine-carrying police, but the galleries were packed with celebrities who matched the London counter-trial in their brilliance and fame. Göring arrived over an hour late, indicating the contempt felt by the National Socialist gods for the feeble court which was the highest in the land. Göring always dressed in a style which (he believed) fit the occasion. This day he strode into court dressed in the dirty-brown uniform of an SA leader.

Everyone leaped to his feet, and every German present snapped the Hitler salute. The President of the court bowed stiffly to Göring and said, 'You could not be deprived of the right to express yourself under oath concerning accusations and slanders which have been directed against Your Excellency from certain quarters, particularly in the so-called Brown Book, regarding the subject matter of this trial'. Here was open licence for Göring to ignore the rules of evidence and launch a blistering harangue! For three hours he ranted against the accused, screaming obscenities, and extolling the Nazi legions who had crushed the communist hordes in the very nick of time. The Reichstag Fire had come as an unpleasant surprise, he said, 'I was like a general who had planned a big attack and who was forced through the action of the enemy to change his plans. I knew at the time that the communists had to act in three or four weeks – at the latest at the general election – and I wanted to await this occasion and destroy them at one blow. It was my firm intention to destroy them in such a manner that the entire leadership would have been wiped out through the insurrection. With the help of the Storm Troopers and the Hitler Guards we could have destroyed communism entirely for the benefit not only of Germany but of the world. The fire entirely upset my plans. My intention was to hang Van der Lubbe that same night. I only did not do it because I thought he might help us catch his accomplices. It was natural that in the heat of the moment some mistakes were made'. With studied contempt General Göring said, 'I personally should not have cared at all about refuting the grotesque allegations in the Brown Book that my friend Dr Goebbels conceived the plot to set fire to the Reichstag and that I carried it out – it is absurd! Though we National Socialists were against the parliament, we used strictly parliamentary means to gain our ends. Violent methods we left to the communists! The fight between Nazis and communists was between two opposite philosophies, that of reconstruction and that of anarchy'. The court must determine who was guilty. 'This trial is going to end. I shall find the guilty and punish them!'

It was an eloquent speech and vigorous despite its length. When Göring had finished, Torgler and the Public Prosecutor asked a few minor questions. This was the eye of the storm. Dimitrov rose to his feet, as one newspaperman put it, 'with as much unconcern as if he were about to cross-examine an insignificant grocer or publican from Neukölln'. An expectant hush fell over the courtroom, and Dimitrov slowly began to needle Göring with insignificant questions, probing and testing his adversary. Then Dimitrov imperturbably reached under Göring's guard and asked: 'On 28th February, the morning papers published a statement or an interview by Minister President Göring on the Reichstag Fire. This report alleged ... that the fire had been started by the Communist Party, that Torgler was one of the culprits, and that the arrested Dutch communist Van der Lubbe carried his passport and a membership card of the Communist Party on his person. How could Minister President Göring know at the time that Van der Lubbe had a Communist Party membership card on him?'

Göring fell for the trap. He answered

that he got his information from the police. 'In case you don't know,' he said, 'I have a police force to do that sort of thing and – in case you don't know that either – the police search every criminal and – in case you don't know even that – they report their findings to me'.

Dimitrov flicked aside Göring's attack and pressed home: 'the three police officers who arrested and searched Van der Lubbe all agreed that no Communist Party membership card was found on him!' Deeply humiliated, Göring was unable to think up an effective reply.

Dimitrov probed again: 'As Minister President and Minister of the Interior and as Reichstag President, did you immediately take steps instructing the police to apprehend Van der Lubbe's accomplices?' (Göring: 'Yes, naturally!') 'And the Minister takes full responsibility for his police?' (Göring: 'Indeed!') 'I ask, what did the Minister of the Interior do on that night and the day afterward to trace Van der Lubbe's path from Berlin to Henningsdorf, his refuge in Henningsdorf, his acquaintance with two other people there, and thus discover the accomplices?'

Göring retorted, 'I'm a Minister, obviously, not a detective hunting tracks, but I do have my police, and I let them take care of these paltry details. After all, at the instant it became clear that Van der Lubbe was the culprit, the entire investigation belonged to the court, not to me. I merely gave the orders to undertake the examination with the greatest possible speed and care'.

Dimitrov continued, 'Afterwards, as Minister President and Minister of the Interior, did you announce that the communists were the arsonists?' (Göring: 'Precisely!') 'That the German Communist Party with the help of Van der Lubbe and other foreign communists were to blame?' (Göring: 'Precisely!') 'And didn't your declarations influence the police investigation and later on the judicial investi-

gation, so that they were led away from discovering the true Reichstag incendiarists?'

Göring was brandishing his arms: 'I know what you're trying to do! The police were given orders to pursue all angles from the very start, regardless of where they led, no matter what the clues! But I am not a police officer! I am a responsible minister! All I had to decide was whether it was a civil crime or political crime! To me it seemed a political crime, and it was my opinion that the criminals could be found in *your* party! And when all the evidence in this court is considered, my estimation remains just as accurate! If I did influence the investigation, then it was in the right direction!'

The Nazi minions who were scattered through the courtroom screamed their approval in a chorus of delight, but Dimitrov hushed them with a snap of his fingers and a contemptuous sneer, 'Yes, of course, bravo, bravo, bravo! Does the witness realize that this criminal party of which he speaks rules the sixth part of the earth, the greatest and best country in the globe, that the Soviet Union has diplomatic, political, and economic ties with Germany, and that its economic contracts give thousands of German workers food to eat?'

In the words of the Reuter correspondent, Göring was 'literally dancing with rage and shaking his fists wildly, while a frenzied stream of abuse poured from his lips'. Above the uproar in the courtroom Göring screamed, 'What happens in Russia does not interest me! I have only to deal with the German Communist Party and with foreign crooks who come here to fire the Reichstag! I'll tell you what the German people know! You are a communist scoundrel who came to Germany to set the Reichstag afire! And now you behave with absolute impudence in the face of the German people! Ahhh! I did not come here to be accused by you!' (Dimitrov: 'You are a witness.') 'In my eyes you are nothing but a scoun-

Goebbels fared little better than Göring against the wily Dimitrov

drel, a crook who belongs on the gallows!'

Through the shouting the President of the Court could be barely heard crying for order. Göring was white with anger, but Dimitrov smiled with hate. 'I'm quite satisfied,' he said, 'Are you afraid of these questions, Herr Minister President Göring?'

His great lungs nearly bursting, Göring roared, 'Out! Out with you, you crook!' As the horrified Bench finally reacted, Dimitrov was hustled out. But Göring flung out a last bellow: 'I'm not afraid of you at all, you thief! I'm not here to be questioned by you! You'll be sorry! Just wait till I catch you if you ever come out of prison!'

The mad scene was over. Göring calmed down enough to point out bitterly that after three hundred years the English were still burning effigies of Guy Fawkes, who had tried to blow up Parliament. 'No trial was held then,' said Göring (erroneously). Foreigners ought to ask themselves

how they would feel if Germany interfered with foreign legal problems! Nevertheless, the Western press drew lessons from the day. The *Manchester Guardian* concluded, 'Those who desire to understand the workings of the Nazi dictatorship and the events of the last nine months will brood long on the whole of this strange, repulsive, and deeply significant performance'. The German newspapers were, of course, on Göring's side and failed to report his most outrageous remarks, but for the benefit of others the *Deutsche Allgemeine Zeitung* published an article written by Dr Sommerfeldt, Göring's press secretary. It said in part, 'The fire is and remains a piece of knavery designed to unloose civil war. If the foreign press refuses to understand this, it must bear in mind the known attitude of General Göring'. The threat was real, but it sounded hollow. Dimitrov had won a fearful battle. But the announcements of a new contest had already been published. On 8th November Dimitrov was to meet Dr Goebbels!

The Nazi Minister of Propaganda

and Enlightenment had keenly observed the battle between Dimitrov and Göring. Goebbels was Göring's chief rival, and he hoped to win points with Hitler by a star performance against Dimitrov. Goebbels had no wish to repeat Göring's mistakes. Goebbels arrived punctually and with a benign look at the reporters. The electric tension was allowed to subside, and Goebbels simply answered the questions put to him by the President of the Court during almost three hours of testimony. Goebbels answered at length but his answers were intricately argued. It was obvious that the clever little doctor was doing everything possible to protect his story. He tried to concentrate upon communist terrorism in the past, and he explained in detail what he had done in the period up to the fire. Frequently punctuating his remarks by jokes, Goebbels seemed relaxed and quiet. The audience responded accordingly. None of his testimony materially advanced the progress of the criminal case against the defendants, but unlike Göring the criminal case was of little concern to Goebbels. After all, Goebbels had not been nearly as conspicuous as Göring in institutionalizing Nazi terrorism. As a result Goebbels could take a more detached viewpoint than Göring could afford. But he repeated the same argument used by Göring: the communists had probably burned the Reichstag so that they could blame it on the Nazis. Why should the Nazis burn the Reichstag when they could have routed the communists at any time?

The subdued attitude of the witness helped the efforts of the Court President in keeping a tight rein on Dimitrov. Consequently, many of Dimitrov's questions were disallowed, and the fiery Bulgarian was continually threatened with expulsion.

Dimitrov began his cross-examination of Goebbels on a light note, but he soon asked if it were true that Goebbels had made a radio broadcast accusing the communists and Social Democrats of joint complicity in the Reichstag Fire. It was a vicious question. If Goebbels were forced to admit that the Social Democrats had no part in the fire, then the Minister opened himself up on two flanks: he would have to admit that the government had acted upon incomplete or erroneous knowledge, and he would have to admit that the government might have been just as precipitate and possibly as ill informed in accusing the communists. Goebbels, however, avoided the pitfall: 'I will gladly answer this question. I have the impression that Dimitrov wants to do some propaganda for the Communist Party before this court. I know what propaganda is, and he need not try to throw me out of my calm by such questions. The connection of the socialists with the communists was a fact. If we accuse the communists, we do not forget their close relationship with the Social Democrats'. However, later on Goebbels contradicted himself by answering a question from Torgler with a remark that 'The obstinacy of both the Communist and Socialist Parties was so great that they would rather be ruined separately than defend the existence of their parties together'.

Dimitrov next concentrated upon Nazi terrorism, since Goebbels had spent much of his testimony on attacking the communists for their violent record. Dimitrov asked the Propaganda Minister whether it was true that a number of Nazis had been condemned to death before 1933 on charges of bombings. Goebbels replied, 'It is possible that outsiders were sent as provocateurs into the ranks of the Nazi Party to instigate such outrages'. Dimitrov pursued this line of questioning by pointing out that political murders had long been common in Germany, taking the examples of Karl Liebknecht and Rosa Luxemburg. Goebbels snorted, 'We might as well talk of Adam and Eve. When those murders were committed, our movement had not even been born!'

Similar niggling comments seemed to win more debating points for Goebbels than for Dimitrov, but Goebbels finally realized that the cumulative effect of implicating one terrorist crime after another with the Nazi movement was subtly but surely undermining the Nazi case.

Eventually, Dimitrov soothingly inquired, 'Has not the Nazi Party passed an amnesty for all terrorist acts committed by Nazis?' Goebbels made the mistake of saying, 'The National Socialist Party repudiates terrorism. If our men defended themselves against communist terror, and committed their acts for the salvation of the German people, then we should not leave them in prison. It is self-evident that we passed an amnesty for them'. Dimitrov clearly had strung the Reich Minister between the two poles of foreign and domestic propaganda. To satisfy one he was unable to satisfy the other. For the moment Goebbels struggled on, saying, 'I am merely answering Dimitrov so that the world press cannot say that I remained downcast and silent. I have given reason and answer to greater men than this little communist agitator'.

Dimitrov, however, was closing quickly. He said, 'All of these questions arise from the political case against me. My accusers alleged that the Reichstag Fire was meant to overthrow the German Constitution. What Constitution was in force on 30th January and what on 27th February?' Goebbels replied: 'The Weimar Constitution, for better or for worse! It was legal and we recognized it as such. What changes in it were made we reserved for ourselves, not for communists! I consider that constitutional changes are necessary!' But by this time Goebbels, too, was angered by Dimitrov. The Bulgarian closed the net, saying, 'That is clear proof that you have no respect for the German Constitution!'

Justice Bünger was incensed: 'Leave the constitution alone!'

But Dimitrov had already gone on. 'Do you know, Minister,' he asked, 'that your fellow Nazis in Austria and Czechoslovakia also have to work illegally and make illegal propaganda with false and coded addresses and correspondence?'

Goebbels spat back, 'It seems you want to insult the Nazi movement! I will answer you with Schopenhauer – "Every man deserves to be looked at, but not spoken with"!' And Dimitrov was content.

After Göring and Goebbels, the Court became far more indulgent toward Dimitrov. After all, if Hitler's two right-hand men could not break this rugged communist genius, how might the court hope to control his outbursts? The justices gradually regained their composure and the spectre of the *Völkischer Beobachter* faded. Dimitrov himself seemed to welcome the change, and for the remainder of the trial his behavior generally improved. Soon, the frosty haughtiness between the lawyers, the bench, the court bailiffs, and the

Left: Count Wolf von Helldorf confronts Van der Lubbe at Leipzig in order to answer the charges of *The Brown Book*. *Above:* Van der Lubbe gives evidence

defendants (except Van der Lubbe) thawed, and a kind of camaraderie developed within the close confines of the Leipzig chamber. As Douglas Reed noted, 'Dr Bünger at times became almost paternal in his altercations with Dimitrov; Dimitrov was occasionally seen roaring with laughter at some joke he shared with his police custodians'. Certainly Dimitrov was granted tacit permission to say things that would have had him excluded from the courtroom only a few weeks earlier. For example, on 2nd December when the court placed a minor cramp on Dimitrov's style, he almost wistfully reminded the judges that he would far rather be free and fighting for communism at home than sitting in a foreign courtroom. 'This soup which you have cooked for yourself, Mr Prosecutor, probably does not taste very good any longer. Because I sit here innocent, therefore, I defend myself as well as I can.' And at another moment that same day Dimitrov caused gales of laughter when he startled a communist prosecution witness with the remark, 'Why isn't this witness under arrest?'

Perhaps most remarkable of all was President Bünger's wry comment, 'Dimitrov, a foreign newspaper has said that it is you who are really conducting this trial. I must object to this, but you will see that your behavior does make this impression on public opinion. You must submit to my authority, and I desire you to limit yourself to asking simple questions from here onward'.

To which Dimitrov replied, 'As defendant, I acknowledge only one superior, and that is the President of the Supreme Court. But I ask my superior to grant me the chance to defend myself and discover the truth.'

Such passages would have been unthinkable in the period before Göring and Goebbels barged into Court. Much of the difference lay in Dimitrov's realization that despite all the show, the Nazis had proven unable to lay a single legitimate charge at his feet.

With that assurance, and with the knowledge that he had already gained one of the greatest propaganda coups of any age, he could relax. Yet he was still more than capable of pricking the hides of the unfortunate justices and Prosecution, as when he said on 5th December, 'In my opinion the witnesses heard in the political section cannot be regarded as satisfactory. On the one hand, they are police officers. Far be it from me to insult officials, as I am often accused of doing. It must be admitted, however, that officials are to a certain extent dependent and that their testimony is not therefore entirely free'. Dr Werner was just beginning to look round in angry amazement when Dimitrov went on. 'Yes, Mr Prosecutor,' he said, 'I know that you and those who give you your instructions –' (The President: 'What do you mean by that?') '– the German Reich and the German Government', smiled Dimitrov, continuing, 'On the other hand the testimony of political prisoners from gaols and concentration camps cannot be regarded as entirely objective since such men are often subject to severe moral pressure.' The Prosecutor was obviously upset, so Dimitrov grinned impishly, and said, 'Is it not true that many German officials before 30th January served earlier governments with the same loyalty and devotion as that with which they now serve the Hitler Government?' But Dimitrov was never again thrown out of court after his confrontation with Göring.

The sole remaining defendant in court was, of course, Van der Lubbe. An endless stream of witnesses testified verifying his wanderings throughout the country before arriving in Berlin. Others told of seeing him in Spandau, in Henningsdorf, in Neukölln, and scores of other places throughout greater Berlin. Cross-examination revealed that many of these witnesses were liars, thieves and bums, but when the kernels of evidence were fully sifted what remained substantiated Van der Lubbe's con-fession. Witnesses came who had seen him in Neukölln, the welfare office, the Town Hall and Imperial Palace fires. All of his other activities in the greater Berlin area were established with ease. The police reports were, again, methodically examined. Witnesses to the Reichstag Fire itself were called over and over.

Van der Lubbe endured these things, but he had become mostly indifferent, sullen, bored, or occasionally amused. He knew what the penalty would be. He knew his execution was inevitable. The pompous rituals were meaningless to him. He did not care to participate.

There were moments in which Van der Lubbe showed his macabre sense of humor in other ways than his fits of giggles. When, for example, the court was belaboring the question of where Van der Lubbe had gone after leaving the police shelter in Henningsdorf, Van der Lubbe had at first refused to answer. But the Court President, Dr Bünger, became exasperated and repeated, 'Where were you?' As the court strained forward to hear the reply, Van der Lubbe murmered half-audibly, 'With the Nazis'. There was a dead silence in the courtroom, and the faces of the justices were tinged with fear. Finally Dr Bünger asked the interpreter if that was really what Van der Lubbe had intended to say. 'Yes', replied the interpreter. The disbelieving justice's jaw dropped further. Turning to the defendant again, he asked, 'With whom, did you say?' And this time Van der Lubbe said, 'No one'. Only with great difficulty did the court find out that Van der Lubbe had merely been one of a group of bystanders watching a Nazi parade!

It was not that he was incapable of speaking out in court; on some occasions Van der Lubbe spoke at length and quite coherently in fluent German (although his accent was difficult to follow). The court appointed an interpreter, Herr Meyer-Collings (much to Van der Lubbe's disgust), who told the court on 6th December as the trial was coming to a close, 'It is very strange, but Van der Lubbe does not speak at all like an ordinary Dutch worker but uses a remarkably educated vocabulary, though he sometimes has difficulty in expressing himself.'

On several days Van der Lubbe spent hours arguing with the court over the long delays and complications. As he said on 23rd November, 'This is *my* trial. I alone am the guilty one, and I want the verdict, whether it is twenty years or death. But at least decide! The whole trial has become so involved because you keep wanting to bring out the symbolic meaning of it all. There obviously was no conspiracy, no collective signal. In the meantime I am not at all happy with the food and the clothes. You could at least give me some clothes that might fit me correctly. What you are doing is a betrayal of the police and a disgrace to the Communist and National Socialist Parties. All I ask is for a verdict.'

Van der Lubbe even took on Dimitrov when the Bulgarian said, 'The President has emphasized, in my view correctly, that the fire was too complicated to have been started by one man'. Van der Lubbe interrupted Dimitrov hotly: 'But it was all so simple! It was perfectly easy to set fire to the Reichstag! The Plenary Chamber must have been easily combustible. But while the fire was a perfectly simple matter, what was made afterward is another story. That *is* complicated. The act of firing is extremely clear, but the question of who could be blamed afterwards has been complicated by politics'.

And when Dr Bünger reminded Van der Lubbe that they had just heard another fire expert say that the Plenary Chamber fires could not have been done by one person, Van der Lubbe retorted, 'That is the personal opinion of the fire expert! The Plenary Chamber must have been more flammable than the experts believe. The

The Chief Public Prosecutor, Dr Karl Werner, gives the President of the Court, Dr Bünger, an affidavit

fact is that I did set it on fire with only my jacket'.

The President: 'Do you mean to say that you kindled each fire on each individual seat in the Deputies' Chamber?' (For the President assumed that there were such fires on those seats – which was most improbable.) Van der Lubbe: 'I never asserted that I laid *those* fires!' The President: 'Well then, who did lay them?' Van der Lubbe: 'I don't know. I was far below.'

Obviously the mental faculties of Van der Lubbe remained unimpaired – when he chose to use them. No 'half-wit' would have caught the distinctions between the various fires in the Sessions Chamber and their importance. And no moron – even a lunatic moron – would have cut off Dimitrov in mid-sentence after watching that wily Bulgarian for over eight months at close quarters.

At last all the evidence had been heard, and on 13th December 1933, the summing up by the Prosecution commenced. Dr Werner, the Chief Public Prosecutor, began by declaring that 'with extraordinary accuracy all the facts have been hunted down which could possibly lead to clearing up the case'. In a plain reference to the National Socialist press, Werner said, 'There may be people who have been impatient at these long proceedings, but this special care was due to the gravity of the matter at issue. The attack on the Reichstag was not only an attack on one of the best-known artistic [sic] monuments of recent times but also on the German people. It was the signal for the enemies of the German State to rise and destroy it and to set up a dictatorship of the proletariat instead.' He bitterly attacked the *Brown Book* as 'a filthy work of propaganda'. In a long speech in which he devoted a great deal of time criticizing the findings of the London Commission of Inquiry, he said, 'It did not produce any material, although I requested it to put such material at my disposal. And when I saw the report of their proceedings, I was not surprised. They admitted that the evidence they had was necessarily incomplete, and in this case it was a ridiculous piece of arrogance to frame a verdict on the strength of it.'

The Deputy Prosecutor, Dr Parrisius, then described Van der Lubbe's past as leading from one form of fanaticism to another against the social structure. He suggested that if Van der Lubbe had succeeded in a spectacular way with his fires at the Welfare Office, the Town Hall, and the Imperial Palace, all Berlin would have been in a panic even before the Reichstag Fire. Van der Lubbe's adventures in Neukölln obviously seemed intended to establish contacts with the large communist strongholds there, but the Deputy Prosecutor admitted being unable to confirm this. Dr Parrisius said that Van der Lubbe's descriptions of how he had entered the Reichstag and what path he had taken once he broke inside could be accepted as truthful. But no one could believe that alone he could have set the fires in the Sessions Chamber. Probably Van der Lubbe's accomplices had stayed hidden until the discovery of the fire and then slunk away in the

excited crowds afterwards. Anyone, but especially a Reichstag Deputy, said Parrisius, could have carried the flammable liquids into the Reichstag 'in a briefcase, as the liquid could have been contained in rubber bottles, which were probably consumed in the blaze'. Van der Lubbe himself had been a mere dupe: 'Everything suggests that he is obsessed with the idea of going down in revolutionary history as an immortal hero'.

The next day the Prosecution continued its closing statements on the remaining defendants. Dr Werner pointed out that all of the accused were communists, so the question was whether the communists stood to profit from the crime and whether they had secretly participated in or planned the fire. The answer, he said, was yes on both counts. Not only did it appear that they had planned the work, but when it had failed to spark a communist revolution, the German Communist Party had blamed the fire upon the National Socialist Government.

As for Torgler, he was seen in the Reichstag with Van der Lubbe by Karwahne, Frey, and Kroyer. He had also been seen leaving the fire with Deputy Koenen just before the outbreak of the fire. If Koenen had not slipped out of the country, said Dr Werner, he would be in the dock alongside the other defendants. Torgler's efforts to escape the blame 'had completely broken down'. The fact that he had slept that night at the home of the Secretary of the Reichstag Communist faction, Kühne, proved that Torgler was trying to hide. When everything was considered, Werner said, 'I come to the conclusion that Torgler had taken part in the Reichstag Fire in some manner or another', even though it could not be proven how this was done.

After a short adjournment, the President of the Court made a strong appeal to Dimitrov not to sneer while the Chief Prosecutor was speaking. Dimitrov answered that he found amusing much of what Dr Werner had said before the break. Then the Prosecutor launched into his summary of the case against the Bulgarians. He alleged that Dimitrov had taken a strong interest in German political affairs. He had entered the country with a counterfeit passport and was using a disguised name. Popov, too, had participated in German affairs during 1932, and the Russian witnesses whom Popov called to support his alibi were 'not in the least worthy of belief'. On the other hand, the National Socialist waiter at the Bayernhof Restaurant, Johannes Helmer, must be discounted, since Van der Lubbe could be proven to have been in the Netherlands during the time Helmer allegedly saw him with the Bulgarians. Obviously Helmer's testimony provided the only essential 'bridge leading to the Bulgarians'. If Helmer's statements broke down upon examination, then there was no convincing proof that the Bulgarians had any complicity in the Reichstag Fire.

Then the Chief Prosecutor demanded death sentences for Van der Lubbe and Torgler. He asked the court to acquit Popov, Tanev and Dimitrov for lack of evidence. There were no cheers. Van der Lubbe had fallen asleep in his chair. Torgler's face was a complete blank. The Bulgarians, including Dimitrov, said nothing.

After closing speeches by the Defence Attorneys, Torgler and Dimitrov were granted the privilege of a last appeal before the Supreme Court. Torgler's speech was reasoned and relatively low-keyed in keeping with his character. Dimitrov's speech was extraordinary, even by his standards, and he attacked virtually everyone in the courtroom (except his two fellow Bulgarians), the police, the State, and the political parties (except the communists). This was his command performance, and no one present ever forgot it. As usual he was blunt, forceful, and passionate. The German and foreign press quoted from it for weeks afterward, and it was finally served up again in *The Second Brown Book* by Münzenberg and Katz.

But the most distinguished speech

Torgler's lawyer, Dr Sack, speaks at the Leipzig Trial

of all was Dr Sack's closing address. He was far more subtle than Dimitrov but just as ringing. His stroke.of genius was in seeming to angrily denounce the *Brown Book* and the attacks on the Supreme Court by the foreign press, but actually he subtly insinuated to the bench that it must prove itself free from 'fear or favor' by acquitting Torgler. Then with magnificent courage Dr Sack (although a Nazi lawyer) venomously attacked the Emergency Decree of 28th February which Hindenburg had signed and which launched the Hitler Terror. He repudiated the legality of the decree, its destruction of the constitutional guarantee of *nulla poena sine lege*, and its unconstitutional imposition of *ex post facto* law. Under both German and Roman law, he declared, the Emergency Decree was invalid. He said he had come to defend Torgler the man, not Torgler the communist, but he had come to respect them both as honorable men. After tearing apart the Prosecution case of Torgler's alleged 'complicity in some manner or another', Dr Sack made a stunning appeal for justice which may have turned the tide for Torgler and which left the court gasping for breath: 'It was our leader Hitler who said,'God forbid that any German had a hand in this crime''. And God be praised, Torgler the German is innocent'!

After a week during which the court retired to consider the sentences, the accused were brought before the bench two days before Christmas to hear the verdict. The President of the court rose in the hushed hall and the prisoners grimly waited. Facing them, Dr Bünger said,

'Let the accused stand up! In the name of the Reich I pronounce the following verdict. The accused Torgler, Dimitrov, Popov and Tanev are acquitted. The accused Van der Lubbe is found guilty of high treason, insurrectionary arson and attempted arson. He is sentenced to death and to the perpetual loss of civil rights. The costs of the trial will fall, according to the verdict, upon the convicted man, the remainder to be borne by the Treasury of the Reich. IN THE NAME OF THE LAW!'

It was all over. Justice was served. The Supreme Court had shown its independent voice for almost the last time before expiring in the quicksand of the Third Reich. The absurd findings of the preliminary hearing were dashed to pieces. More than 250 witnesses had been called, twice the expected number. Over 10,000 pages of testimony had been filled. Some 7,000 wax recording discs had been cut.

The guilty man was beheaded with a shorthandled axe by the State Executioner, who was dressed in top hat, tails, and white gloves. The other prisoners were eventually freed. Torgler remained in Germany and survived the war to live in West Germany. The three Bulgarians after some delays were whisked away to the Soviet Union and became Soviet citizens. The *Brown Book*, which Dimitrov had called 'the sixth defendant', achieved legendary success. In Germany, the National Socialist press used the Reichstag Fire and continued to say long after the trial that (in the words of the *Leipziger Neueste Nachrichten*), 'Only Hitler was able to save the world from the Bolshevist hydra'. In the West, an anti-Fascist crusade had been launched with incalculable results, and *The Times* (London) said, 'Not within memory, and perhaps never, has the concern of one country been so spontaneously the concern of all. Who fired the Reichstag? If it were fired by Nazi hands, there is no evidence of it before the court. If by communists, they fired it only to make a Nazi triumph'. But while the great princes of Nazi and communist propaganda fought out their battles in the world's headlines and history books, the insignificant wretch who had caused all the fuss died miserably, alone.

Epilogue

In the course of the present book, the author has argued that there is no real doubt that Van der Lubbe was actually the sole architect of the Reichstag Fire. The evidence surely makes this the only acceptable opinion at the present time. Yet there will always remain a remote possibility that further findings or admissions may crop up to invalidate or amend the story as we now understand it, and so we should allow a tiny twinkling of doubt to remain on the periphery of our conclusion. In all fairness there is still a great debate in some quarters about who fired the Reichstag. After four decades the question retains a highly political flavor. Few events from the troubled history of Germany in the 1930s have evoked so much acrimony and lasting political discussion.

Before 1959 almost everyone accepted the verdict of the London countertrial and, with minor reservations, the two *Brown Books* by Katz and Münzenberg. However in the late 1950s historians became aware of the researches of Dr Fritz Tobias, a Social Democrat, once member of the post-1945 State De-Nazification Commission and later a director of the Security System of Lower Saxony. In 1959–1960, the controversial findings of Tobias were given wider publicity on the pages of *Der Spiegel* and a number of other West German newspapers and magazines. Finally, in 1962, Tobias published the definitive study of the subject, a massive volume of over 700 pages. Tobias proved once and for all, he hoped, that Van der Lubbe was a solitary arsonist, that neither the Nazis nor the communists participated in planning or setting the fire, and that both sides later distorted or covered up the truth for conscious political gain, because of stupidity, or through blind ideological prejudice. Most historians, including the present writer, accept Tobias' findings.

But a minority of historians persist

Who fired the Reichstag ? The political and historical controversy continues

in the original *Brown Book* version or close variants of it. Communist historians are still united in tightly adhering to the old ideologically required dogma: The Nazis Did It. A few non-communist Western historians and politicians also seem to fear that Tobias has opened a Pandora's Box which might exacerbate the ideological passions of our present generation, and some of these critics apparently want to blame the Nazis for everything which had gone wrong in Germany since 1918. For these people the suggestion that a radical anarcho-communist acting alone set the German parliament building aflame is met with outright disbelief, horror, and cries of heresy.

At this point the present-day discussions of the Reichstag Fire become patently political. In 1969, for instance, the 'European Committee for Scientific [sic] Research into the Origins and Consequences of the Second World War', submitted the interim conclusions of its specially constituted sub-committee of 'The Commission of Inquiry into the Origins of the Reichstag Fire' before a press conference on 17th October at the Lutétia Hotel in Paris. The report was submitted by members of the commission which included Walter Hofer, director of the Institute of History at Berne; Jacques Delarue, a French historian; Simon Wiesenthal, head of the Jewish Documentation Center and famous for his search for Martin Bormann; and Edouard Calic, a Jugoslav historian. Receiving the report was a select panel of celebrities including Willy Brandt, the new Chancellor of Germany; Pierre Grégoire, President of the Luxembourg Chamber of Deputies; and André Malraux, former French Minister of Culture. The meeting before the press was chaired by Grégoire, but one senses that most of those present were there as window-dressing. The 'Secretary' of the commission, Calic, was apparently the motive force behind the scenes.

What purpose drew all of these glittering personalities together on the stage? Surely the 'Origins of the Reichstag Fire' were unimportant to them except insofar as it related to their immediate political purposes. And those purposes were far from academic: they simply wished to dash the Tobias version to pieces.

According to the 1969 Commission, it was impossible for Van der Lubbe to have single-handedly set the Reichstag aflame. They said that the order to destroy the Reichstag came from the highest quarters inside Nazi Germany. Hitler was probably actively involved, but Goebbels and Göring were mainly responsible for conceiving the plot. It was, said the Commission, probably Göring who dreamed up the idea in the first place. A few elite members of the government were brought into the game, including Wilhelm Frick (Reich Minister of the Interior), Hans Franck (Hitler's legal advisor), Alfred Rosenberg (Chief Party ideologist – remember Sefton Delmar's testimony?), and a small handful of others. The technical preparations were directed by Himmler and Heydrich. Dalüge, the SS Chief-of-Staff in Berlin, and Rudolf Diels, the director of the Secret Political Police, were the operational supervisors responsible for making sure that no one could trace the crime back to its origins. Special flammable substances were introduced into the Plenary Sessions Chamber by the joint SS and SA Commando Force, who came in through the tunnel system from Göring's House. Van der Lubbe and the other men, said the report, were brought to trial after being specially chosen for the operation in advance so that the communists might be accused of the crime. For all of this astounding information, the Commission of Inquiry into the Origins of the Reichstag Fire (1969) then told reporters, there was documentary evidence which would be published before the spring

Dimitrov shortly before his death

'Dust to Dust': The Reichstag in ruins in 1945; destruction began by fire was completed by war

of 1970. Unfortunately little more has been heard of this 'Commission with the high-sounding title' as *Die Zeit* called it, although it did manage to produce a few relatively uninformative letters-to-editors in European newspapers. However, the implications of the commission's allegations were rather spectacular, for without substantiating its accusations, it has come perilously close to libeling Tobias, his supporters and his sources while ignoring grave questions about the commission's own credibility. Like the International Commission of Inquiry into the Origins of the Reichstag Fire (1933) headed by Secretary Otto Katz, Secretary Edouard Calic's Commission in 1969 failed to publish its documentary evidence. But Calic, also like Katz, did reveal some conclusions in a book which appeared while the Commission was in session. Since it is likely that we shall have little better methods of evaluating Calic and his Commission (unless the long-awaited documents do finally appear in cold print), a few comments are justified concerning Calic's book.

As an exercise in folly and pretension, Calic's book would seem to have few peers in the historiography of the Reichstag Fire. It claims to present totally new information, and it claims to be far the most definitive

The Reichstag after the Third Reich

study of the subject, yet the sources remain for the most part obscure (where he makes the wildest accusations) or trivial (where he lists them). But far more damning is his failure to confront vital issues raised by Fritz Tobias. The comparison of the two books is instructive in how to write a good book and how to write a bad one. Tobias documents everything he says by citing chapter and verse. Calic does not. What this means is that the one is inviting comparison or analysis of his sources – and the other is hoping his readers will trust him. Considering the rather sordid distortions and inventions that have plagued histories of the Reichstag Fire before, Calic's apparent invitation for us to trust him on faith alone is asking rather more than seems remotely reasonable. Incidentally, the same unusual reticence to disclose his sources of information or reveal the documents upon which his narratives are based is characteristic of Calic's other excursions into historical writing as well.

Hopefully two examples of·Calic's remarkable agility with the improbables of history in *Le Reichstag Brule!* will suffice to indicate the point: we learn in great detail that one of Calic's primary sources, upon whom he assiduously relies for the 'fact' that the Nazis were involved, was a Berlin corner barber, who told Calic about what some Nazi gossips

told him while sitting in the barber's chair nearly forty years before: i.e., that there was more to the Reichstag Fire than met the eye! What do we know about the garrulous barber? Nothing. What do we know about the idle gossip in his chair? Nothing? Is this the kind of source upon which one should rely in placing a case for conspiracy against the bar of history? Absolutely not. Or let us take another stirring example. Calic places full confidence in the startling 'revelations' he records from a self-important baker who believed the prattlings of our old friend Otto Grothe, who was plastering the baker's establishment one day during the war after bomb damage. By the time the baker heard him, Grothe was insisting that Göring was behind the Reichstag Fire. Calic fails to mention that those who had attended the trial in Leipzig and heard Grothe's testimony about secret meetings held by communist plotters on the afternoon of the Reichstag Fire, had already come to realise that the babbling Grothe was a pathological liar, one who in fact had displayed a remarkable facility for changing his story from one moment to another in mid-stream. In fact Grothe, as we have seen, narrowly escaped being arrested by the Supreme Court for blatant perjury. On such hearsay evidence from unqualified witnesses Calic builds what may loosely be termed his 'argument'. Finally, there are two more observations concerning Calic's book. Firstly, it has been published in Italian and French but not in German or English, in which every other serious study of the Reichstag Fire has been printed. If the book were worthwhile, one may presume that it quickly would have found its way into one of the two languages wherein all important research in the subject has hitherto been conducted. Secondly, one looks in vain for any reviews of Calic's book in relevant academic or popular journals – a matter of some surprise considering his sweeping claims and the widespread interest shown both by historians and the popular press in the question of who burned the Reichstag. *Die Zeit* suggested that the 1969 Commission (*not* Calic's book, incidentally) might open a great battle between historians when and if the Commission revealed its sources and evidence. On the one side, said the newspaper, would stand a British-Dutch-West German Defense-Pact of historians favouring Tobias. On the other side would stand a French Luxembourg-Swiss Aggression Pact of those who wished to prove that the Nazis did it after all. There would be no pardons, and *Die Zeit* only hoped that all the combatants would fight for Truth and nothing but the Truth.

One cannot hope that we shall ever ever know the whole truth about the Reichstag Fire. Perhaps in future Calic, his Commission, or someone else may bring forward additional information refuting the main points made by Fritz Tobias and his supporting legions of historians and documents. Until then there can be little doubt that dispassionate historians must insist that the available evidence indicates that only Van der Lubbe was guilty. No one need suggest that Calic, his Commission, or the others who look to find a Nazi plot in the steam tunnels are communists. On the contrary we should appreciate the sophisticated accomplishment of the original inventions of Katz and Münzenberg (and the tantrums of Hitler, Göring, and Goebbels), which provided a ready explanation for a mysterious event that occurred under a barbarous regime. Conservatives and liberals alike took the fictions of the Comintern Paris *Apparat* into their life-blood. This should give one no cause for dismay; it merely proves that one should carefully subject evidence on important historical questions to the most careful possible scrutiny – especially when the apparent findings of other investigators fit too comfortably into ideological preconceptions, whether in 1933 or tomorrow.

Bibliography

A Study in Tyranny Alan Bullock (Odhams, London)
Trail Sinister Sefton Delmer (Secker & Warburg, London)
The Path to Dictatorship: 1918-1933 O K Flechtheim *et al* (Anchor Books)
To the Bitter End Hans Bernd Gisevius (Jonathan Cape, London)
My Part in Germany's Fight Joseph Goebbels (Hurst & Blackett, London, 1935)
Prelude to Calamity: The Nazi Revolution, 1933-1935 Eliot B Wheaton
(Gollancz, London)
The Reichstag Fire: Legend and Truth Fritz Tobias (Secker & Warburg, London)
The Burning of the Reichstag Douglas Reed (Gollancz, London)
Insanity Fair Douglas Reed (Jonathan Cape, London)